CINEMA '76

CINEMA '76
Edited by David Castell

Published by
Independent Magazines (Publishing) Limited
Bridge House, 181 Queen Victoria Street
London EC4V 4DD. Telephone 01-248 3482

© Independent Magazines (Publishing) Limited 1975
ISBN 0 904894 00 2

Printed in England by
Exallprint Limited, Tunbridge Wells

Dustjacket illustrations:
Front, colour: James Caan in Rollerball; black and white, left to
right: Valerie Perrine in Lenny, Steve McQueen in The Towering
Inferno, Clint Eastwood in Thunderbolt and Lightfoot, Elizabeth
Taylor in Ash Wednesday. Spine: Robert Redford in The Great
Waldo Pepper. Back, colour: Barbra Streisand in Funny Lady; black
and white, top to bottom: Charles Bronson in Death Wish, Julie
Christie and Warren Beatty in Shampoo, Dustin Hoffman in Lenny,
Paul Newman in The Sting; left to right: Burt Reynolds in W W and
the Dixie Dancekings, Robert Redford in The Great Waldo Pepper,
Gene Wilder and Peter Boyle in Young Frankenstein, Ian Bannen and
Sophia Loren in The Voyage

*Cinema '76 is dedicated with grateful thanks to the
readers of Films Illustrated, whose loyalty made this book possible*

CONTENTS

Foreword

Oliver Reed

In the last six years I have watched the growth of Films Illustrated from a tiny weekly called Films in London, to what it is now — an extremely polished, well produced and highly respected magazine. Now the same people who thought up Films Illustrated are embarking on their first annual, Cinema '76. There's every reason to hope and believe that they'll make the same success with this venture as they have done with the magazine.

The reason I've always had a soft spot for Films Illustrated is the way it balances the British scene with the important events going on outside these islands. I wish I could say that for the bulk of the industry I work in. The general attitude is far too insular.

For example, I make most of my films abroad. This is not because I want to, but because I have to. The glamorous image that most of the public have about film stars on location couldn't be further from the truth, believe me. Mostly it's just bloody boring. Every time I leave my home and everything that entails, it's a terrible wrench. But, as I've said before, you've just got to go where the bread is, otherwise there's no work.

The other encouraging aspect of Films Illustrated is the way it reflects change. Our attitude to change in the film world is unbelievable. For years we resisted it, and then suddenly we fell over ourselves trying to flow with the tide. For an actor though, you have to be given the opportunity to change. Ken Russell gave me mine in those BBC documentaries on the composers Debussy and Rossetti.

Until then I'd been working mostly for Hammer Films playing Teddy boys or werewolves. Those were great for paying the rent, but hardly likely to pick up the awards. No-one bothered to find out that behind that mask of make-up I had to use for the werewolf, there was an actor dying to break out. No-one thought I had a soul but, as my ex-wife and my publican know, I spent a lot of time in those days wandering around Wimbledon Common singing Negro spirituals. Then came Ken Russell to intellectualise me, followed closely by Michael Winner to please my bank manager. Both Winner and Russell have taken a lot of stick in the press about the films they made. True, some of Michael's movies were geared solely for the box office, and may have been over-violent, and Ken sometimes doesn't seem to know when to call a halt, but both men have remarkable personalities. Nothing is impossible to either of them, and that's an attitude not only I admire, but so too do their backers. That's why they never stop working.

4

At the moment the film industry in this country is in a shocking state. Even Michael Winner and Peter Collinson have been forced to work abroad, along with several others. So, apart from Russell's films, the only films being made here are Carry Ons or low key children's features.

It makes me angry when I read the trade press each week to find the audiences going down and down. Where have they gone, they ask? It's not the audiences that have gone away, but us in the industry. If we can provide the right product they will surely come flocking back.

My next ambition is to produce films myself. I hope that by the end of 1976 my production company will be in full swing. My aim is to bring romance and adventure back on the screen. *The Three Musketeers* and *The Four Musketeers* proved that, properly done, these kind of movies are real winners (sorry, no pun on Michael intended).

Let's get the families back in the stalls. That's my dream for the rest of the '70s, and I hope that *Cinema '76* can help me realise it. The people who have compiled this book are young, ambitious and, just in gambling on the new venture, they've proved they are willing to lay their reputation and this money right on the line.

Good luck: I hope you succeed.

Stages in Oliver Reed's career. Top: as a gang member in The Angry Silence. Centre: in The Brigand of Kandahar. Bottom: burning at the stake in The Devils; Opposite: as Bismarck in Royal Flash

PS: Thank God you didn't ask Richard Harris to write this foreword. You'd never have had any space left for articles.

Cops and Robbery

John Williams

*Opposite:
Gene Hackman,
playing 'Popeye'
Doyle again
in French
Connection
Number 2*

More films have been made about cops during the '70s than possibly about any other subject. The cinema — and particularly the American cinema — is increasingly obsessed with the practice of law and order, at a time when corruption in the highest levels of public life has become commonplace. Cops have been portrayed as goodies in the '70s, but not nearly as often as they used to be in the days of the Keystone Cops or our own perennial PC Dixon. Indeed, straightforward, cop-as-hero movies like *An Investigation of Murder* (*The Laughing Policeman* in America) have become the exception, so that it is rather comforting to see Walter Matthau re-affirming faith in the traditional movie-policeman.

Cops have, rather, been bad, and increasingly more so. Two of the most important films made recently — *Serpico* and *Report to the Commissioner* — are true stories of corruption within the New York and Los Angeles Police. Cops have also been indifferent, amusing, and downright stupid. They've also taken the law into their own hands. Ultimately, so have civilians, like Charles Bronson in the sinister *Death Wish*, believing in a private means of revenge. Cops have been ubiquitous, at a time when the most indigenous of movie genres — the western — has declined, run out of steam.

The conclusion is a fairly obvious one: cops have taken over, at least in cinematic terms. Films like *Walking Tall, Dirty Harry* and *The Stone Killer* are successors to the western myth.

But so many of the recent offerings have been totally mundane, contributing nothing more or less to our enjoyment of the cinema than the B-westerns of old. That there are so many B-cop movies around is a clear sign of the times, for the modern cop-movie genre is already waning.

The films that have provoked discussion are, in many cases, quite exceptional movies. *Serpico,* for example, is an almost definitive exposé of corruption. *Dirty Harry* is a parable for our times. *The French Connection* and its sequel offer possible answers: that a good law-and-order-man has got to be zealously tough to cope with our civilisation. While *Electra Glide in Blue* achieves the ultimate: a myth-shattering movie that absorbs much of the pure western form.

But why the boom in cop movies? Films do, frequently, anticipate real-life happenings (*Marooned*, for example). But more usually they reflect trends. The tragedy of the Vietnam war contributed very largely to the unprecedented decline in public morale which took place in America in the late '60s and early '70s. By coincidence (or possibly

8

as a result), the Establishment rotted. Within a very short space of political time, America accepted with muted disbelief, the resignations of its Vice-President, and its President. And in smashing the rotten fruit, she could not get to the core quickly enough. Almost daily, hitherto honoured names like Kissinger and Rockefeller were accused over one matter or another.

America was not alone, of course. Britain was rocked by the Poulson affair, and then shocked by the attempted disappearance of one its MPs, a former government minister. The Prime Minister of India was convicted of corrupt electoral practice, and when her opposition noisily demanded her resignation, she promptly threw them into jail. The Chancellor of West Germany, the highly respected Willy Brandt, had to resign over responsibility for a spying affair.

At the same time, personal violence increased the world over. Football supporters wrecked towns, trains and people. The world which Anthony Burgess and Stanley Kubrick so brilliantly visualised in *A*

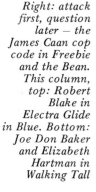

Right: attack first, question later — the James Caan cop code in Freebie and the Bean. This column, top: Robert Blake in Electra Glide in Blue. Bottom: Joe Don Baker and Elizabeth Hartman in Walking Tall

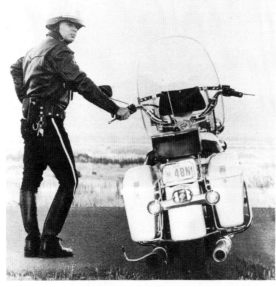

Clockwork Orange, became far less of a myth, and far more of a reality. "As to supporters' violence," commented The Sunday Times, "much superficial nonsense has been written. How, after all these years can people still see it as an isolated phenomenon, rather than a symptom of general sickness ... Society at large should be relieved and delighted that football is paying its debts, carrying its burden." Movies certainly reflected this trend. *The Mean Machine* and *Rollerball* echoed the violence of sport. On the cop front, queues formed for hard pictures like *Magnum Force.* Audiences lapped up violence, and the new cinema of escapism — the disaster films — simply underlined the lemming-like intent. Even the pure escapism of *kung-fu* pictures appealed mainly to a desire to see people being bashed about.

"Inevitably the methods used by intelligence services to check terrorism involves work that is disagreeable. Telephones will have to be tapped. Letters must be opened. Informers must be paid. *Agents provocateurs* must be planted. Gossip must be noted and

filed." No, not a scene from a sci-fi movie or the speech of a pro-Fascist politician, but a quote from a pamphlet published by a backbench Conservative MP, Philip Goodhart, dealing with the Ulster problem. Trust has gone, possibly never to be regained. And the inevitable backlash is in full flow. Similarly, movies have followed corruption exposés with a sickening flood of law-and-order statements, and many of these advocate lawmen taking things into their own hands. *Walking Tall* is probably the most reactionary of these backlash movies.

There is a rather better-made film, *Freebie and the Bean*, which succeeds in making us laugh when we should be horrified. Freebie (James Caan) and Bean (Alan Arkin) are two cops who are both vicious and irresponsible badge-holders. But they are funny — very funny. I can remember laughing hysterically when they succeeded in driving their car off a freeway into the *third* floor flat of an aged couple. I can also remember, vividly, being sickened by the closing fight sequence when Bean is all but mutilated by his transvestite victim. But if *Freebie,* directed by Richard

Above: Al Pacino in Serpico. Left: Gene Hackman and Roy Scheider grill a suspect in The French Connection

11

Rush, is a smooth blend of the genre's characteristics over the past few years, then maybe *All the President's Men* will provide the full stop. This, the story of Watergate, was snapped up by Robert Redford who is teamed with Dustin Hoffman as the two Washington Post reporters who uncovered the scandal. Alan J Pakula directs, but whether or not America is ready to re-live the affair remains to be seen. The lemmings are very close to the sea, but are they quite ready to make the final jump?

Very few cop movies have tried to pose serious questions. As Dilys Powell (The Sunday Times) said in her review of *Serpico*, "The cinema is so busy with car chases: violence, and background realism that it has no time for sympathy." Films like *Cops and Robbers, The Seven-Ups* and *Busting* are intended as entertainment, and viewed from the distance of London, they succeed in being so. As Gavin Millar (The Listener) said of *Cops and Robbers:* "The cheerful amorality of Donald E Westlake's bright script doesn't aim to bring down the government." Unfortunately, this is exactly what many American critics cannot take. Andrew Sarris (Village Voice), for example: "... the fantasy element which we assume in all movie plots actually encourages us to forget not only the daily revelations of police being tripped up by the penal code, but also the imputation of improprieties to our only President and our only Vice-President.

"The trouble is that shakedowns and such would remind us all too quickly of the real New York City Police Force which managed to misplace the heroin confiscated from the French Connection. Actually, it is the loving complicity of its audience which makes *Cops and Robbers* the cinematic equivalent of Watergate." Sarris is probably over-reacting to Aram Avakian's film, but his point is quite valid, and Cliff Gorman's and Joe Bologna's cops have much in common philosophically with Elliott Gould and Robert Blake in *Busting*. Written and directed by Peter Hyams, *Busting* is a light-hearted frolic whose heroes are quite incapable of achieving even the simplest of arrests, though the film did make the point that "it is as much life inside the station house as out on the street that grinds cops down, makes them petty and vicious." (Jay Cocks, Time).

Corrupt, dirty, or just plain inefficient, these are formula cops in formula movies with their obligatory car-chases and other familiar trappings. David Robinson, reviewing *The Seven-Ups* which was directed by Philip D'Antoni (who produced both *Bullitt* and *The French Connection*), wondered whether audiences ever question "how the chasing automobiles can always so reliably find a fruit stall, a bridge and generally a railway crossing complete with express in their way, yet never encounter traffic jams, culs-de-sac, etc." In the film, a dumbfounded policeman is moved to say at one point: "Nobody cares any more." The implication is a clear one.

Caring is what *Serpico* is all about. Sidney Lumet's film is the true story of one Frank Serpico's discovery of corrupt practices in the New York Police Force. Even so, Dilys Powell was dismayed that the subject "seems to surprise nobody, and that leads one to consider the change in public reaction to the moral or social problems presented in fiction form.

"When in the early 1930s Paul Muni appeared in *I Am a Fugitive From a Chain Gang* horrified spectators would assure one another that it was all true and that there were indeed chain gangs in the Deep South; the film became a matter for public discussion. I don't know what you have to do in the cinema today to excite moral reproach ..." Miss Powell's attitude is perhaps pessimistic. Nigel Andrews (The Financial Times) thought that: "For once, the film's makers seem more interested in the film's moral theme than in the scenes of eye-catching violence used to illustrate it." And Pauline Kael (The New Yorker) attacked Lumet and writer Norman Wexler for imposing "their own careless cynicism on Serpico's life." It's an attitude, says Miss Kael, that "goes with the popular new pose about how America is coming apart at the seams and *should* — a pose in which corruption is some sort of retribution for Vietnam and everything else." But if, as Frank Serpico himself claimed in an interview with Miss Kael, "the truth was so much better," the film was nevertheless a remarkable attempt to present the truth to a society which often has difficulty in believing it.

Cops had rarely been corrupt in the long history of movies. Cops were, indeed, very rarely over-indulged. In the '20s, they were sources of amusement; in the '30s, the private eye claimed all the limelight, and the poor cop, though always there to perform the final arrest, was little more than a cypher. Later films gave cops a human side (*Laura,* for example) while *The Naked City* (1948) and *Detective Story* (1951) took their problems seriously. Welles' *Touch of Evil* was even more accurate. But then during this growing-up period, there was always the western. With Watergate and Vietnam, America reached an emotional and historical

Opposite: Charles Bronson in Death Wish

Cop comes a cropper: Clint Eastwood fails to master the art of motorbike riding in the climax of Magnum Force

watershed, and suddenly her heroes and legends were no longer quite so interesting.

The best film to emerge about it all is really Don Siegel's *Dirty Harry,* featuring Detective Harry Callahan as portrayed by Clint Eastwood. This hard, apparently amoral fable about a cop who holds the law in contempt and prefers to take his own action, was misunderstood in many quarters. A number of leading American critics looked at the film's superficial gloss and decided it was a right-wing hymn to law-and-order. But Derek Malcolm (The Guardian), got to the real point of Siegel's masterpiece: "... it recognises more clearly than *The French Connection* that in the predatory world of big-city America you can't send a puppy to chase wolves. If you create that sort of brutal society, you have to live by its rules absolutely."

Siegel's theme is that the cop and his target are outside society, isolated in their vicious world. In defending Siegel from the attacks of Pauline Kael, Vincent Canby and others, Paul Nelson (Rolling Stone) wrote: "In a way, Harry is the logical genre continuation of the timeless American western myth — the lone-gunfighter-as-hero, and the proud son of John Wayne, James Stewart, Gary Cooper, and Henry Fonda — but the difference is that in today's cities, more violence is required, not less." Nelson concludes that "Eastwood (as Harry) never forgets his moral purpose. Harry doesn't so much beat the system as prove himself an individual man of value different from it — he makes a separate peace. True, the firing of the final bullets may be moral only because he doesn't miss, but then he knew he wouldn't all along, didn't he?"

Dirty Harry was in many ways a western in the style of the '40s, but it dealt in the realities of living in 1971. It is a stark film which stands out almost exclusively from its contemporaries. "Sociology, huh? Well, just don't let your college degree get you killed" is exactly the kind of Callahan-ism that upset the critics. But it's valid.

Dirty Harry (one suspects for the wrong reasons) was enormously popular with audiences, another factor which angered its opponents. Inevitably its success lead to a sequel being made, *Magnum Force,* in which Eastwood again played Harry Callahan. Sadly, however, Siegel did not direct. This job went to Ted Post, something of an expert at sequels, and the script was by John Milius (who has since directed *Dillinger* and *The Wind and the Lion*) and Michael Cimino (whose *Thunderbolt and Lightfoot* is itself about a Vietnam war veteran, also played by Eastwood, who turns against the society

Gian Maria Volonte in Investigation of a Citizen Above Suspicion

which has rejected him). For the critics of *Dirty Harry,* the sequel was a purification, but to most people, *Magnum Force* was opportunist, exploitative rubbish. Derek Malcolm found it "almost unspeakable — far nearer the pornography of violence than the despised *Straw Dogs.*" And Alexander Walker (The Evening Standard) found that it made attractive "the notion that the law is so incapable of remedying society's ills that vigilantes are the cure."

Magnum Force is, to my mind, an evil film. David Castell (Films Illustrated) summed it up: "...a total product of the climate it pretends to condemn. It is such an unthinking film that I find the notion (of box-office success) even more frightening than the legal corruptions on which it pretends to frown."

Walking Tall is another nasty film. It is the story of a real-life Sheriff (note the direct parallel with the old-time western) who decides to clean up his home town. There is much violence and much preaching about the values of personal retribution but, to borrow Derek Malcolm's concluding sentence: "God save us from ever becoming a society so twisted that it takes a man like him to unravel the knots." Joe Don Baker played Sheriff Buford Pusser and the film was again so successful that the producers made a sequel. The horrifying aspect of films like *Walking Tall* is the nature of their backlash qualities. In responding to the apparent cry for law-and-order movies, certain film-makers have produced fairly responsible, though dull, movies. Richard Fleischer's *Precinct 45 — Los Angeles Police* (*The New Centurions* in America), for example, manages to contain possible excesses, though it is patently too pro-cop for its own good. Of course there has to exist an efficient Law Force in our modern society. But, as Michael Kerbel (Village Voice) said: "...a more objective presentation, including at least a hint of police fallibility, would have made more palatable the argument that police are only human." The film ranged widely over the areas of urban crime: drugs, prostitution, and so on; but the examples it presented were treated as pieces of entertainment, something to be laughed at. Considering the story was by Stirling Silliphant, who wrote the firmly liberal *In the Heat of the Night* as well as the

balanced TV series "Naked City", *Precinct 45* was too ordinary a disappointment.

But if this is rebound material, films like *Walking Tall* are totally excessive. And beyond these, we have the ultimate, urban vigilante presentations such as Michael Winner's *Death Wish* and Ossie Davis' *Gordon's War*. Cops, they say, are incapable of controlling or preventing modern crime, and it is up to the victim to seek his own, highly personal revenge. In *Gordon's War*, the "hero" returns from Vietnam to find his wife dead as a result of the drugs forced on her by the pushers of the ghetto. The film really says two things: that while "the boys" were away fighting for honour in Vietnam, America went sour; and that in doing so, she totally rejected her returning "heroes." America does not wish to be reminded of the fiasco of Vietnam. One can hardly blame "the boys" for reacting to this treatment, and they have done in a number of post-War movies like *Thunderbolt and Lightfoot* (see above) and *My Old Man's Place*.

Michael Moriarty played the proud son returning home in this latter film which was, however, totally uninspiring in movie terms. The same actor is the star of a new anti-corruption film, *Report to the Commissioner*, which has its roots in Vietnam in the sense that the hero's father is an ex-cop and his eldest son intends to follow the same career but is killed in the War. It is left to younger brother Moriarty to step, most reluctantly, into the vacant shoes. Following in father's footsteps is a medieval concept, but the film says a great deal about the moral conflict current in America. When our hero unknowingly kills a policewoman on "undercover" duty his superiors attempt a cover-up: he must be punished for their mistakes. The whole thing is very sharply reminiscent of Watergate, and the boy's innocence is carried forward to the punishment cell: "I killed a girl. They've got to kill me." It is, incidentally, based on a true story.

But back to vigilantes. The world's number one box-office star is, apparently, Charles Bronson. He enjoys enormous popularity in places like Japan and Italy rather than in America, but *Death Wish* is not merely a star vehicle. It is a total vindication of the revenge-outside-the-law theory. Bronson's wife and daughter are attacked, the one killed, the other savagely raped. He decides to take personal revenge by shooting as many of the muggers, layabouts and urban casualties of the New York parkland as he can get away with. But beyond that, the police, when they catch up with Bronson, allow him to go free because by now, he is a

public hero. Many critics liked *Death Wish*, as certainly did audiences. I have very strong reservations. To suggest that the forces of law and order might comply with a situation like this seems to be dangerous and irresponsible. And I also think that the film's main objective is to entertain. Put the two together and you have a very dubious mix. *Death Wish* is more subtle than, say, *Walking Tall*, but my feelings about both these movies are entirely coincident.

Outside America, only one film of any serious merit is worth mentioning. Elio Petri's *Investigation of a Citizen Above Suspicion* also happens to be one of the best films here discussed, a powerful and brilliantly directed and performed story of a police inspector who commits murder and then literally dares his department to expose him. He is beyond the law because he forms a major source of its establishment. Gian Maria Volonte played the lead role in this clearminded message-movie which, as Derek Malcolm points out, says "that the vaccine of authority is repression, no matter how 'democratic' that authority calls itself." Dilys Powell says that this is "something basic to Fascism, the elevation of authority over moral law."

But if the Italians succeeded in one film in saying more about corruption than the rest of the world in dozens, it is to the American cinema that one returns for any kind of conclusion. Messages and meanings have been discussed in some detail. What has not been said is that most of the cop genre films are made in the name of entertainment, and so to a final consideration. How successful is the genre in entertaining?

Apart from *Electra Glide in Blue*, which is a highly watchable movie, my affections lie with William Friedkin's *The French Connection*, and, for different reasons, its sequel, directed by John Frankenheimer. Gene Hackman is such a fine actor that it would be difficult to dislike anything he did, but his portrayal of the dedicated, often abused, often sad, 'Popeye' Doyle, is *the* highlight of our era of cop movies. Admittedly both films deal with many of the message points: corruption, individual interpretation of the law, and so on. But they do so totally *within* the context of an entertainment film. Friedkin's film also had possibly the best of the car chases, while Frankenheimer's goes one better still, as Hackman runs along Marseille harbour walls in pursuit of the boat carrying his enemy, Fernando Rey. 'Popeye' Doyle is a tough character, and a bitter man, but he never gives up — and that statement would in itself seem to sum up the Cop of the '70s.

Turning on to TV Movies

David Quinlan

Have you seen the latest films made by Jack Smight, Lamont Johnson, George Cukor, Andrew V McLaglen, Gordon Hessler or Norman Panama? If the answer is no, the odds are that you haven't been watching much television lately.

For all these men, and more besides, have been putting their talents to the improvement — and in the last two years that improvement has been considerable — of the once-despised TV movie, those films specifically made for television consumption.

Time was, when the very words TV movie were sufficient to make one reach for the Off switch. Hopelessly padded out to reach the commercially required length of seventy-two or ninety-three minutes, the initial examples, made in 1967, were slow, uninspired and for the most part made by journeyman directors used only for turning out fifty-minute stories for the TV medium.

A plethora of local California scenery would usually indicate where a commercial break was to be inserted. And the actors were mainly "second-eleven" players who had never quite managed to reach stardom in the cinema of the '50s and '60s, or who had briefly flourished at the end of the studio contract system, and had subsequently found freelancing such hard graft that they

had drifted into television series, either in guest spots or as regular stars.

Even when reputable directors and actors did work for TV, the results, such as Don Siegel's *Stranger on the Run*, with good performances from Henry Fonda and Dan Duryea, were, despite being better than average for the time, still below the standard of their makers' work for the cinema. The scripts lacked telling dialogue, the budget showed signs of economy. And even *Stranger on the Run* moved in fits and starts, the demands of commercial breaks hampering Siegel's fluency with a storyline.

The films came mainly from the hands of Universal, although some were made also by Paramount, MGM and Warners. And the net results very much resembled slightly below-average double-bill fare that one might expect from Universal-International in the mid '50s.

In 1969, it was hard to see a future for the television film. The whole idea seemed about to fizzle out. But the realisation that TV had not been selective enough about subjects and scripts, that fifty minutes was not the same as seventy-two, and far from ninety-three, was beginning to dawn.

A film called *Fear No Evil*, made in 1969, and first shown in Britain in 1970, was not only the first TV film I can remember

mystery with characters being taken over by people from the past, which featured Barbara Stanwyck, Richard Egan and Kitty (then Katherine) Winn; and *How Awful about Allan*, a who's-doing-what-to-whom with Anthony Perkins, Julie Harris and Joan Hackett. The latter was directed by Curtis Harrington, later to lure Gloria Swanson to the little screen to star in his *Killer Bees*.

Although the quality of horror scripts for TV was to go down in the early '70s, it remained above that of those offered by the cinema, specialising in the terror behind the door rather than the overt and often hybrid horror presentation in *Dracula A D 1972*, *And Now the Screaming Starts* or *The Legend of the 7 Golden Vampires*.

The censorship imposed in American TV (you won't hear any four-letter words either, in contrast to British TV plays and films) may have had something to do with this, and may have even helped the development of the TV film to its present literate and interesting state.

Not that the old horror favourites were forgotten: *Scream of the Wolf* is only one variation on the werewolf legend, and the splendid Gale Sondergaard made a welcome return to the macabre in *The Cat Creature* (again directed by Curtis Harrington). *Wolf* was directed by Dan Curtis, who made *House of Dark Shadows* and the Palance *Dracula*.

Meanwhile, the more elderly of the great Hollywood stars were beginning to bite at some of the more interesting carrots TV was offering. Edward G Robinson gave a stand-out performance in *The Old Man Who Cried Wolf*, while Van Heflin was equally note-worthy in *The Last Child* (made just before his death).

But it was the great female stars who really opened the gates, to permit TV films to seize a whole new category of actor. Barbara Stanwyck, the late Susan Hayward, Joan Crawford, Joan Bennett, Jane Wyman, Judith Anderson, Olivia de Havilland, Rosalind Russell and Maureen O'Sullivan all chanced their arm in the new genre — and few of them got their fingers burned. Miss Russell and Miss O'Sullivan co-starred memorably in a rare TV comedy-thriller, *The Crooked Hearts,* which also featured a rare appearance (as a charming but homicidal rogue) by Douglas Fairbanks Jnr.

And Miss Bennett joined the chiller crowd in Reza Badiyi's *The Eyes of Charles Sand*, which was about premonitionary vision, and definitely not for the nervous.

Even Bette Davis finally succumbed, to the lure of Gordon Hessler's *Scream Pretty Peggy*, with talented Sian Barbara Allen

enjoying, but also the first to fully exploit the exciting possibilities of the small screen in the enclosed world of the chiller. Lynda Day plays a girl who keeps a nightly tryst with her dead *fiancé*. Neither she, nor Louis Jourdan who plays the psychiatrist trying to help her, have ever been better. And the climax, involving the shattering of a bewitched full-length mirror, is something of a real eye-opener.

Some highly effective essays in the genre followed, notably *The House That Wouldn't Die*, a very frightening haunted house

giving Miss Davis hot competition in the bulging eyeball stakes as a young student who becomes housekeeper to a sculptor obsessed with depicting evil. Bette is his equally weird mother, and Hessler gives the grimly melodramatic proceedings that follow quite a kick.

With the stars came the directors, notably improving such things as pace, editing and atmosphere, especially in thrillers, with the exception of series of films, such as *McMillan and Wife, Columbo* and *McCloud*, many of which started promisingly, but were getting very blunt and tired by the time their third season came round.

By the mid '70s, TV movies could be said to have mastered every genre with the exception of the epic. In 1973, the number of TV movies produced in America exceeded the number of films for the first time. Despite the fact that the length and concentration of effort and talent required to produce a *Godfather* was not yet available to them, a larger portion of TV films — perhaps one in ten, something approaching the old Hollywood ratio — was proving excellent, sometimes even compulsive watching — better than their cinematic challengers.

As well as chillers and perceptive dramas, TV was now proving especially adept at detective dramas set in the past, capturing not only the look of an era, but the feel as well.

Robert Day's *Banyon*, which took 1937 as its year, set a good example, with the help of a script by Ed Adamson that made gentle fun of the crime movie screenplays of the time, without losing any tension in the process. But particularly good was *Goodnight, My Love*, directed in 1972 by Peter Hyams, who made the underrated *Busting* for the cinema a year later.

Goodnight, My Love, set, unusually — and immaculately — in 1947, takes most of its action at night, and sets its characters in corners, or cramped, confined conditions, such as narrow staircases. Its heroes are two fairly down-at-heel detectives, played by Richard Boone and the dwarf actor Michael Dunn, a contrast which gives rise to some crackling dialogue. On one occasion, when Boone gets beaten up, Dunn says, indignantly: "What'd you expect me to do — punch him in the knee?" But Dunn does have his uses — standing behind a door through which bullets are expected to come, and do, over his head (both complain bitterly about the damage done to their office), and identifying a killer by his shoes.

The "heroine" is a double-dealing, Lauren Bacall-style blonde, played by Barbara Bain, who eventually gets shot to death in a tense

scene inside a cinema; and the central character in a plot more complicated, if anything, than *The Big Sleep*, is Victor Buono, playing Julius Limeway, a fat, white, luminous slug of a man, forever sitting at the same corner table of his plush night-club and consuming endless quantities of snails.

Exciting in a different, totally exhausting way, was *Hi-Jack*, directed by Leonard Horn, whose previous work, including *The Magic Garden of Stanley Sweetheart*, with Don Johnson, and *Corky*, with Ben Johnson,

Top: Olivia de Havilland in The Screaming Woman. Bottom: Richard Boone, Michael Dunn and Barbara Bain in Goodnight, My Love

21

35114 ABC 12-19

has been largely unseen in this country. A cast headed by David Janssen and Keenan Wynn doesn't exactly drag one screaming to the TV set, but Horn draws an unusually forceful performance from one, and an unusually understated one from the other, as two truck drivers. Janssen's licence has been suspended, Wynn has a weak heart.

Out of the blue, they are offered the reinstatement of Janssen's licence plus a big fee to move a secret government cargo from California to Texas. What they don't realise is that they are merely a decoy, to be harried and shot at by enemy agents, while the real government cargo is elsewhere.

Horn never lets up on the subsequent breathless pursuit across desert terrain, creating an exciting, hard-hitting and tautly edited action film much after the style of Hough's *Eyewitness* or Spielberg's *Duel*. Like these, the highpoint is reserved for the last reel when Janssen, having left Wynn behind, fights a desperate battle with a helicopter in a pulsating, nail-biting duel with an explosive ending.

When the drivers finally arrive in Houston, their contact (William Schallert) gives them their money — several thousand dollars. "Not enough," snarls Janssen sinking his fist up to the elbow in Schallert's stomach. He and Wynn walk away.

The most prolific of all well-known directors working in television today is undoubtedly Jack Smight (although Paul Wendkos runs him a respectable second).

Smight's best TV movie is probably *The Screaming Woman* in which, as usual, he was well served by a good cast that included, in this case, Olivia de Havilland, Joseph Cotten, Ed Nelson and Walter Pidgeon. Miss de Havilland plays a frail woman convalescing after a spell in a mental home who discovers, in the grounds of her estate, a woman almost completely buried beneath the earth. She hasn't the strength to get the woman, the victim of an attack, out, and none of the people she goes to will believe her. Her continual visits to the "grave" lead to an eventual, chilling confrontation with the would-be murderer.

This very frightening film (best seen, I think, in black and white) apart, Smight's TV work, including the three-hour version *Frankenstein* shown here in cut version in cinemas, has not matched his films, which include *The Moving Target (Harper)*, *The Travelling Executioner* and *No Way to Treat a Lady*.

Although directors like Smight, George Cukor (maker of the much-acclaimed *Love among the Ruins* with Olivier and Katharine Hepburn), Ben Gazzara (making his director-

ial debut on his friend Peter Falk's *Columbo* series) and Richard Quine tend to take the headlines when they make a TV movie, a group of lesser-known directors, trained in television, have been quietly turning out some very superior fare in recent times. William Graham, Peter Hyams, John Korty, Robert Moore and Marvin Chomsky may not be household names now, but they are surely destined to become better known.

Moore's best television film to date is *Thursday's Game*. Gene Wilder and Bob Newhart play two fortyish husbands who get away from their wives (Ellen Burstyn and Cloris Leachman) once a week at a big poker game. When the poker school breaks up, the two men decide to lie to their wives and continue going out together. The script takes a biting look at both the hearty male friendship and the marriage in which familiarity breeds desperation. Wilder is admirable in a more subtle kind of comedy role than those in which audiences have got used to seeing him.

Marvin Chomsky's rivetting *Mongo's Back in Town* is based on a novel by a convict. You won't hear any four-letter words even in this TV film. But it's as tough as the laws will allow. Joe Don Baker plays (and is very good as) a professional gunman who returns to his home town where his brother Charles Cioffi) is under surveillance by a cop (Telly Savalas) in a counterfeiting case. When his brother is found murdered, Mongo turns sleuth to ferret out the complicated truth. The dialogue packs a punch all the way and the girls in the plot, Sally Field and Anne Francis, are both more than decoration.

If asked, however, most people would probably vote for John Korty's *The Autobiography of Miss Jane Pittman* (which gained, with *Duel*, the "honour" of being released as a cinema film in Britain) as the best film so far made for TV. Cicely Tyson won an Emmy for her playing of the title role, a coloured girl who lives through a turbulent 110 years and emerges as an aged but spirited civil rights worker in the 1960s whose crowning achievement is to drink from a water fountain previously reserved exclusively for whites.

Korty and teleplay writer Tracy Keenan Wynn also won Emmies, Wynn having gone on to become a director himself on the intriguing, yet-to-be-seen *Hit Lady*, about a professional female assassin, which not only stars, but has a script by Yvette Mimieux.

While the younger directors have been examining the possibilities of the new medium, some of the older brigade seem to have taken a new lease of life from it. J Lee Thompson, for example, has produced his

Opposite: Martin Sheen, the television film's hottest property, in Lamont Johnson's That Certain Summer

23

best work in years with *The Great American Tragedy*, shown over here as *Man at the Crossroads*, and fought shy of by British television, which has tended to play it in off-peak hours.

George Kennedy and Vera Miles play a couple in their mid forties whose cosy and comfortable life falls apart when he quite unexpectedly loses the job (aerospace engineer) that he has been building up for

Top: Yvette Mimieux in the yet-to-be-seen Hit Lady. Bottom: Dennis Weaver in Duel, directed by Steven Spielberg

twenty years. Caryl Ledner's script is perceptive, adult and believable, and Kennedy's first-rate portrayal gets right under the skin of the man at the crossroads of his life.

One had begun to think that James Goldstone would never make another good film after the undervalued *Winning*. But now, for TV, he has turned in *Cry Panic*, a superior, stylish variation on the-body-disappears theme. John Forsythe is a man who accidentally knocks down a pedestrian. But the dead man disappears, and everyone in the town is hiding a secret concerned with him, even the police. Forsythe becomes a helpless fly in a chilling web of events from which there seems no escape.

Andrew V McLaglen has forsaken westerns but stuck to the out of doors. After cutting his TV teeth on a Banacek episode, he came up in 1974 with *Log of the Black Pearl*, a sunken treasure adventure yarn exquisitely shot in colour in waters off Mexico.

But pride of place in the veterans' stakes must go to Buzz Kulik for his affectionate and ultimately moving *Brian's Song*, with James Caan giving a warm and witty performance as the football player doomed to die in his twenties.

TV is certainly making more young directors than actors — although there are notable exceptions. Stockard Channing made a shattering debut in *The Girl Most Likely To*, directed by Lee Philips, whom some may remember opposite Lana Turner in the original *Peyton Place*. Miss Channing plays a very plain, dumpy girl whose features are transformed — into very pretty ones — by plastic surgery after a car smash. She goes after revenge on those who had rejected her . . . in bizarre fashion.

Another new girl is Karen Valentine, a peppy, perky and personable little actress whose several starring roles in TV films include *The Girl Who Came Gift Wrapped*, *The Daughters of Joshua Cabe* and, most notably, Norman Panama's *Coffee, Tea or Me?*, as an airline stewardess with two husbands, one in L.A., the other in London.

Perhaps television's biggest discovery is Martin Sheen, an intense young actor, who had had a long stage career before being hailed as a star "overnight" in Terrence Malick's *Badlands*. A mixture of James Dean and a young Kirk Douglas, Sheen was born in 1940, and didn't film until 1967, in *The Incident*, then repeating his Broadway role in *The Subject was Roses*.

Those weren't released in Britain; neither were other Sheen films, which included *No Drums, No Bugles* in 1971.

Television boosted his stock sky-high in the '70s, with two films discussed below. He has also recently made a TV movie called *The Story of Pretty Boy Floyd*, which takes a graphic, detailed and sympathetic look at the famous Oklahoma outlaw-gunman of the '30s, whose connections with outlawry date back to the James Brothers.

Sheen's career, however, is tied up with the last director in our survey. Only four films made for television get a four-star rating in the current (1975-76) edition of "Movies on TV". And two of them were directed by the same man. His name is Lamont Johnson. Although not a young man (he was born in 1920), this former actor only made his first film in 1967.

In 1972, he combined with Sheen for the first time on *That Certain Summer*, the first TV film to deal exclusively, and tastefully (although Tom Gries' *The Glass Cage*, originally made for TV, had touched on it) with homosexuality. Hal Holbrook gives a painfully poignant portrayal of a married homosexual whose fourteen-year-old son (the sensitive Scott Jacoby from *Baxter!*) discovers his secret. Hope Lange plays Holbrook's ex-wife and Sheen the man with whom he lives.

Johnson then went on to make three excellent, and widely differing cinema movies: *The Groundstar Conspiracy*, a tension-charged science-fiction thriller, with Michael Sarrazin and George Peppard; *You'll Like My Mother*, a skilful horror-comic with Patty Duke and Sian Barbara Allen; and *The Last American Hero*, with Jeff Bridges, as a champion stock-car racer from the sticks, and Valerie Perrine.

Better than all of those was the next Johnson-Sheen TV movie, made in 1974. This time Sheen had solo spotlight in *The Execution of Private Slovik*, which more than ever illustrated the director's flair for making "difficult" subjects watchable, touching and entertaining.

Eddie Slovik was the first American soldier to be executed for desertion since the Civil War. But he is so shocked by his experiences in battle that firing a rifle becomes anathema. He deserts, marries, is eventually recaptured and shot. Sheen's portrayal of the man is magnetic, and complemented by the warm support offered by newcomer Mariclare Costello as his young wife. It's a hauntingly unforgettable performance that tops anything he has ever done before, and should put him up with the Nicholsons and Redfords before the '70s are out.

And the drama of Eddie Slovik, which might be so prolonged in the footage conscious cinema of today, is tightly edited, lovingly made, and heartrending to watch. It is an outstanding film on any level.

More directors of talent, it is hoped, will put their gifts to use in the TV film as the months go by. How nice it would be if someone like Hitchcock, who takes years to set up a bona fide movie, were offered the time, and proper facilities to make, say, two ninety-three minute TV films a year. For the TV film is no longer the poor relation. And such a suggestion is by no means as extravagant as it might seem at first sight.

Top: Joe Don Baker and Sally Field in Mongo's Back in Town. Bottom: Karen Valentine and Richard Long in The Girl Who Came Gift-Wrapped

The Films of the Year

Optimism, excitement, anticipation: these are the key words for 1976. Films like *The Godfather, The French Connection* and *The Sting* were no mere flukes, the last words of an industry that everyone had thought dead. They were the beginnings of a new era.

Never has the cinema passed through such an exciting phase of growth and development. The film-makers at work: Francis Ford Coppola, Steven Spielberg, George Roy Hill, Richard Lester, Martin Scorsese, Mike Nichols, John Schlesinger, John Avildsen — the list is almost endless. Producer-teams like Zanuck and Brown who hit the heights with *The Sting* and are now climbing even higher with *Jaws*. Players like Gene Hackman and James Caan, Barbra Streisand and Liza Minnelli; newcomers like Robert DeNiro, William Atherton and Valerie Perrine. Writers: Tracy Keenan Wynn and Robert Towne, Wilbur Smith — and those who direct like John Milius. The incredible nostalgia boom. Now we look back to the '50s in *W W and the Dixie Dancekings*, the '20s in *The Fortune*, and the cinema's own glittering history. Arthur Hiller is directing Rod Steiger in *W C Fields and Me*; Sidney Furie is filming *Lombard and Gable*.

The cinema now has, without question, the richest history of all the twentieth century art forms. And unusually for a contemporary, emerging art form, it has also entertained the masses in a way that the music, paintings and books of earlier centuries were unable to do. Cinema speaks most easily to its audience because it is an essentially visual form — something which all great film-makers instinctively know.

Television, in terms of entertainment and art, is becoming less of a force, although TV movies are getting paradoxically better in quality. But it is essentially a news medium, a reporting medium. To relax, to escape from the home, to be flipped to another place, another time, another world, people are returning to the cinema.

To the vicious daring of Norman Jewison's *Rollerball*, with superstar Caan. To the pure adventure of *Shout at the Devil*, with Lee Marvin and Roger Moore. To the political full-stop of *All the President's Men* — Redford and Hoffman in the story of Watergate. To Peckinpah's *Killer Elite* with upcoming superstar Robert Duvall. To the romance and pure tradition of *The Story of Cinderella*. To the suspense of *Jaws*.

It is a fantastic era for movies — a thrill era, an excitement era. An industry is being re-generated by talent — and that, more than any other single factor, is the good news for the mid-'70s.

Opposite: Burt Reynolds in W W and the Dixie Dancekings.

27

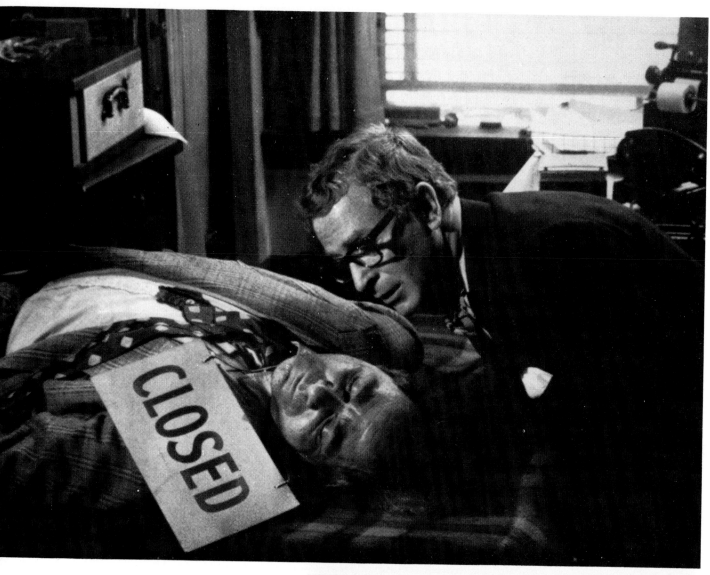

FAT CHANCE

re-introduces Michael Caine to the seedy world of the private eye. Set in the Los Angeles of 1948, the film is based on the novel "Deadfall" by Keith Laumer and co-stars Natalie Wood in her first film for five years. (The Affair was made for television although it was subsequently given a theatrical release in Britain.) Caine's previous associations with the detective thriller have yielded much career success—notably as Len Deighton's spy Harry Palmer in The Ipcress File, Funeral in Berlin and Billion Dollar Brain

KILLER ELITE

*stars James Caan in a violent suspense thriller
involving a CIA plot. Directed by Sam Peckinpah,
whose previous films have included The Wild
Bunch, Straw Dogs and Pat Garrett & Billy the
Kid, the new film is based on a novel by Robert
Rostand, and tells the powerful story of one
man's search for revenge after he has been
betrayed by his best friend. Also starring are
Robert Duvall, Gig Young, Arthur Kill and a
twenty-two year-old Vietnamese beauty, Tania*

THE STORY OF CINDERELLA

is director Bryan Forbes' first musical (and his first film made in Britain since The Raging Moon). The fairy story is set to music by the brothers, Robert and Richard Sherman, whose previous hits include Mary Poppins, Chitty Chitty Bang Bang and Charlotte's Web. As his Cinderella, Forbes has chosen an unknown twenty-two year-old named Gemma Craven who, says Forbes, is the most exciting discovery of his career. Richard Chamberlain is cast as Prince Charming. Other stars pictured on these pages include Annette Crosbie as the Fairy Godmother; Christopher Gable as the Prince's friend and companion; Margaret Lockwood as the Stepmother; Rosalind Ayres and Sherrie Hewson as the Ugly Sisters. Dame Edith Evans plays the Dowager Queen, Kenneth More the Lord Chamberlain, Michael Hordern the King and Lally Bowers the Queen. To find appropriate castles with dreamy spires, the unit travelled to Austria. Near Salzburg they found this dream of a castle, built in the middle of a still lake that mirrored the snow-capped mountains. When the location shooting was complete, the unit returned to Pinewood where craftsmen had created sets of fairy-tale loveliness to complement Julie Harris' costumes and the score

W C FIELDS AND ME
and
LOMBARD AND GABLE

*are two films which the sceptics said
would never be made. Arthur Hiller directs
W C Fields and Me starring Rod Steiger
as WC and co-starring Valerie Perrine.
Jill Clayburgh and James Brolin have the unenviable
and challenging task of portraying
Carole Lombard and Clark Gable
in a romantic drama about the stormy courtship
and marriage of the two great Hollywood stars.
This film is directed by Sidney Furie.*

DIAMONDS

stars Richard Roundtree as The Thief in an exciting story of a would-be diamond heist, with locations that see-saw between London and Israel. Also starring are Robert Shaw as the brains behind the ingenious theft, and Barbara Seagull (previously Barbara Hershey) as the girl. Diamonds is directed by Menahem Golan

ROLLERBALL

promises to be the film of the year, a science fiction adventure thriller set in a savage futuristic society where war has been eliminated and Man's natural instincts for hostility and violence are catered for by the game of Rollerball. James Caan stars as Jonathan E, a battle-scarred veteran of the game—a stubborn, independent spirit whose rebellion against the system of the corporate society becomes a very real threat. Maud Adams (pictured here with Caan) plays the ex-wife who resented his continued involvement in the game. Based on a short story, first published in Esquire Magazine, by William Harrison, the film is produced and directed by Norman Jewison. John Beck plays one of Caan's colleagues, a man who becomes a victim of the vicious sport, and the supporting cast includes Oscar-winner John Houseman, Moses Gunn, Sir Ralph Richardson, Pamela Hensley and Barbara Trentham. The action sequences where shot in the Munich Olympic Stadium where the insurance premiums—against loss of life or limb on the part of the players—were the highest ever paid during the making of a film. Jewison himself believes that the film touches on some of the most pertinent subjects of modern-day life: the increasing brutality of organised sports and the continual lowering of our own thresholds of shock and outrage . . .

JAWS

already looks set to become one of the biggest box-office successes of all time. In its first week of release in America, it took ten million dollars—up on both The Sting and The Exorcist. Based on the best-selling novel by Peter Benchley, Steven Spielberg's film tells of the terror caused when a mammoth, man-eating shark starts attacking swimmers in the waters of a small beach resort community. Roy Scheider, Richard Dreyfuss and Robert Shaw are the three modern-day Davids who seek to destroy the oceanic Goliath. The film was shot largely on location in and around Martha's Vineyard, an island five miles south of Cape Cod. Conditions were often difficult and dangerous for the crew— always uncomfortable. Their difficulties were matched by the fifteen special effects men who worked tirelessly to achieve graphic realism in the capsizing and burning of boats, the tearing apart of piers and the attack of sharks. Their faith and efforts would appear to have been rewarded . . .

ALL THE PRESIDENT'S MEN

stars Robert Redford and Dustin Hoffman as Washington Post journalists Bob Woodward and Carl Bernstein, the reporters whose dogged and fearless perseverance led to the uncovering of the whole Watergate scandal. Directed by Alan J Pakula (whose political thriller, The Parallax View, was one of last year's best films), the film was conceived when Redford himself snapped up the rights to Woodward and Bernstein's novel while it was still in galley form.

SHOUT AT THE DEVIL

is an adventure story set in German East Africa during the days of World War I. It stars Roger Moore, Lee Marvin and Barbara Parkins. Marvin plays an Irish-American adventurer called Flynn Patrick O'Flynn who brushes with the German colonial authorities while poaching ivory. Moore plays Sebastian, a sophisticated and well-educated Englishman who is tricked into joining Flynn's illegal activities. Barbara Parkins plays Rosa, Flynn's beautiful daughter who falls in love with Sebastian and—to her father's outrage—marries him. The film is produced by Michael Klinger, directed by Peter Hunt and based on a novel by Wilbur Smith—the trio who made the successful Gold. Shout at the Devil was made on location in the Transkei, a wild, humid and beautiful coastal region of South Africa—also in Malta

THE FORTUNE

stars Warren Beatty and Jack Nicholson as two out-and-out rogues who scheme to separate an heiress from her fortune. They select Stockard Channing, playing the heiress to a sanitary napkin factory. Director Mike Nichols returns to comedy for the first time since the huge success of The Graduate

QUILP!

is a musical adaptation of Charles Dickens' "The Old Curiosity Shop." Anthony Newley, who plays the title role, wrote the music and lyrics for seven new songs. His co-stars include David Hemmings, David Warner, Michael Hordern, Paul Rogers, Jill Bennett and Mona Washbourne. The film introduces Sarah Jane Varley as Little Nell and Sarah Webb as the Duchess. Quilp! is the third musical based on a Dickens novel: "Oliver Twist" become Oliver! and "A Christmas Carol" became Scrooge. Quilp! is directed by Michael Tuchner for Readers Digest (their previous productions were Tom Sawyer and Huckleberry Finn, both musicals); the dances were staged by Gillian Lynne and Elmer Bernstein wrote the musical score

RUSSIAN ROULETTE
is based on Tom Ardies' novel, "Kosygin is Coming" which, like Frederick Forsyth's "The Day of the Jackal," takes fictional liberties with a factual situation. It is set in Vancouver in 1970 where the fragile East-West detente is about to be cemented by the arrival in Canada of the Russian leader. That's the fact. The fiction element is that the KGB believe a mysterious Vancouver resident is planning to kill Kosygin, and the stage is thus set for a frantic thriller as disaster threatens the fragile peace. George Segal stars and the film is directed by former editor Lou Lombardo. Cristina Raines, Denholm Elliott and Gordon Jackson co-star

MANDINGO

*concerns slavery, incest and the degradation of the Negro in the Deep South of the
1840s. James Mason stars as Warren Maxwell, master of Falconhurst, a slave-breeding
plantation in Louisiana, who has arranged a marriage for his son, Hammond (Perry King),
with cousin Blanche (Susan George). Boxer Ken Norton plays Mede, a pure
Mandingo, highly prized by slave owners for their prowess as breeders and fighters. During a
disastrous wedding night Hammond discovers that his bride is not a
virgin and on their return to Falconhurst he continues to consort with
his negro "bed wench." His abandoned wife, crazed by jealousy and drink, resorts to a series
of actions which threaten to destroy everyone, including herself. Directed by Richard Fleischer.*

THE REINCARNATION OF PETER PROUD

tells of the obsessive search by a young man who comes to believe in his own prior existence. Michael Sarrazin plays Peter Proud, a history professor troubled by recurring dreams. One night his girlfriend wakes him and says he was talking and screaming in his sleep — in a voice not his own. Proud finds himself irresistibly drawn to seek out the people and events of his previous life. Based on the best-seller by Max Ehrlich, the film is directed by J Lee Thompson and also stars Jennifer O'Neill as a woman from the previous life who becomes important to the present. It was made on location in California and New England

The Unkindest Cuts

Clyde Jeavons

The vetting of films prior to their public exposure persists as the last bastion in Britain of the notion of overt censorship of a cultural or entertainment medium. The theatre has been without its blue-blooded blue pencil wielder for eight years now, and even television relies upon internal codes and its "family viewing policy" (which gears programmes to time slots) rather than a formal censorship procedure (as well, ironically, as feeling free to show old X films intact and without fuss).

It is sobering to note, in fact, just how many fingers there are in the film censorship pie quite apart from the British Board of Film Censors and local licensing authorities. The Customs, for example, can prevent films from entering the country, as they did with *Deep Throat;* the police have been known to seize films in mid-exhibition on the whim of the man-in-the-street and even — as in the case of Andy Warhol's *Flesh* — rip them physically from the projectors; distributors and exhibitors have no automatic legal protection, even when they show a film with a BBFC certificate, and will react with caution in the wake of a prosecution; cinema managers are additionally responsible for the enforcement of age restrictions; and even the Festival of Light, the most notorious of

Britain's self-appointed moral watchdogs, has its own film viewing committee.

The events of the mid '70s have done little to clarify or progress the censorship anomalies beyond polarizing the arguments which have raged incessantly since the escalating liberation of the media in recent years. The failure of a private prosecution against *Last Tango in Paris* under the Obscene Publications Act appeared to be a victory for the abolitionists, yet it was only a technicality and not common sense which led to its legal vindication, and the longer-term effect has been to open the way to further prosecutions under archaic Common Law. This precludes both the calling of expert witnesses and the sensible consideration of the work as a whole; only a section — a single frame even — need be found legally offensive for the whole film to stand condemned. This was in fact demonstrated soon after the *Tango* trial by the successful prosecution before a judge and jury of the GLC-certificated Swedish sex-education film, *More About the Language of Love,* which led to fines on the distributor and cinema manager and dismay throughout the exhibition industry and among licensing authorities and liberals alike.

Prior to this, the unwilling censors of the

GLC Film Viewing Board, led by their radical Chairman Enid Wistrich, had tried unsuccessfully to relinquish their powers and free Londoners at least from film censorship. A small majority voted against Mrs Wistrich's motion, and she honoured her earlier promise to resign. Coincidentally, Stephen Murphy, Secretary of the BBFC, also chose this period of turmoil in which to resign. In the ensuing confused and uncertain atmosphere it took the captains of the film industry a full six months to decide upon his successor, and the arrival of James Ferman in Soho Square is perhaps an apt moment briefly to recall the tortuous and often risible development of film censorship in Britain and America.

"The movie," wrote Henry Alan Potamkin, "was born in the laboratory and reared in the counting house. Filthy hands taught it to walk." Just as the first film-makers came rapidly to spot the box-office possibilities of sex and titillation, so were the moral guardians on both sides of the Atlantic quick to sense the potential corrupting influence of the brash new medium of cinematography. The celluloid sex urge found itself fighting a running battle with censorship almost from the day the movies were invented. In 1912 the British Board of Film Censors was set up by the film industry as protection against the powers of local authorities who, through an absurd loophole in the 1909 Cinematograph Act which was intended solely to establish fire precautions in cinemas, found they had a right to control film content. Thereafter, the Board itself exercised such a rigid, paternalistic control over what was permitted on the screen that for forty years characters in British films and foreign imports had no sex life at all, let alone an irregular one. It is highly revealing of the Board's imperious and inflexible attitudes during this period that it was able to ban a film (as it did Germaine Dulac's *The Seashell and the Clergyman* in 1926) on the grounds that it was "apparently meaningless. If there is any meaning, it is doubtless objectionable."

The American movie industry had moved even faster in its eagerness to hold its own censorship reins, forming the National Board of Censorship of Motion Pictures as early as 1909. In 1915, this became the National Board of Review, and in 1922 ex-Postmaster General Will Hays, a dedicated bureaucrat who became known without affection as the "Czar," was invited to clean up Hollywood after a spate of off-screen scandals had rocked the movie capital and fuelled the fires of American moralists and censorship lobbies. He it was who developed the Production Code, which banned every hint of sin, from breasts to blasphemy, and he it was (so it is alleged) who decreed that if a husband sat on his wife's bed (only singles being permitted) then he must keep one foot planted firmly on the floor.

Later on in America, under the stimulus of strong religious factions, the National Legion of Catholic Decency was formed to "rid the country of its greatest menace — the salacious motion picture," and proceeded to snap powerfully at Hollywood's heels for thirty years. This body continues to keep a stern eye on films shown Stateside and still applies its own highly individual ratings (including C for Condemned).

Unlike their British counterparts, American producers — having piously enthroned their own moral guardian — spent the next three decades seeking ingenious ways to deceive his puritanical eye. The strictures laid down by Hays were pretty well the same as those in Britain. As one cynic put it: "Hollywood buys a good story about a bad girl and has to change it to a bad story about a good girl." But Hollywood's moguls developed into masters of sexual disguise and subterfuge. Cecil B DeMille, for example, discovered that whereas a minor bit of hanky-panky in modern Manhattan might end up on the cutting-room floor, if you set an orgy in Biblical times and came on strong with the Christian ethics, you could get away with all manner of fleshly excesses — hence such ambiguous epics as *The Ten Commandments, King of Kings* and *The Sign of the Cross*. As Darryl Zanuck, head of 20th Century-Fox, rightly said: "When you get a sex story in biblical garb, you can open your own mint." Choreographer Busby Berkeley found that putting acres of diaphanously-clad chorus girls into a musical setting hardly raised Hays's eyebrows, no matter how suggestive the routines. Producer Hunt Stromberg, among others (but he is the one who is supposed to have said at a script conference: "Boys! I gotta great idea! Let's fill the screen with tits!"), leaped with delight upon the unwritten law that allowed bosoms to be bared as long as they belonged to dusky maidens and appeared in "serious" documentaries. And, of course, stars like Jean Harlow and Mae West used their own original techniques to ensure that little was left to the imagination even when their mammaries remained buttoned up.

In the '40s Hollywood got bolder, responding to the demand for stronger wartime escapism and the more urgent sexual needs of young America. Howard Hughes challenged the Censor Code by launching Jane Russell's spectacular chest, packed into a

Maria Scheider and Marlon Brando near the dramatic peak of their relationship in Last Tango in Paris

specially cantilevered bra, in *The Outlaw*,
defying the despairing protests of censor
Joseph Breen, who complained to Hays that
he had "never seen anything quite so
unacceptable as the shots of the breasts of
the character of Rio."

Then at last the film industry made its bid
for freedom in both the Old World and the
New. The studio system was breaking down;
the economics of film-making, under
enormous pressure from the formidable
challenge of television, were becoming criti-
cally unstable; the post-war social climate
demanded an airing of more adult themes;
and an invasion of realistic, sexually explicit
foreign films (particularly from France and
Italy whose censors, despite their Catholic
background, had always been more concerned with politics than sex) showed that
integrity and eroticism could be combined
without turning the whole of Western civilisation into a latterday Sodom and Gomorrah.

Slowly but significantly, the Board in
Britain and the Code in America were forced
to accept themes touching upon adultery,
rape, seduction, homosexuality and all the
other realities of the wicked world, in such
milestone movies as *A Streetcar Named
Desire, Baby Doll, From Here to Eternity,
Room at the Top* and *Victim*. Recalling,
perhaps, the liberties taken (and got away
with) by Busby Berkeley in such films as
Roman Scandals and *Gold Diggers of 1933*
and the stir caused by Hedy Lamarr's naked
appearance in *Extase*, the censors continued
to hold out strongly against nudity, creating
ultimately a test case out of the bare breasts
glimpsed in *The Pawnbroker*. There was, if
anything, even stronger resistance to "bad"
language (not so surprisingly when one
remembers the inordinate fuss caused by
Eliza Doolittle's exclamation of "Not
bloody likely!" in Shaw's *Pygmalion* and
Clark Gable's famous line in *Gone With the
Wind*, "Frankly, my dear, I don't give a
damn") leading to bitter in-fighting over the
Molly Bloom monologue in Joseph Strick's
Ulysses (later shown uncut and uncon-
demned on British TV). The '60s, however,
saw even these bastions crumbling, and
British censorship attitudes in particular —
under the enlightened guidance of BBFC
Secretary John Trevelyan — underwent a
radical overhaul which opened the way for
debate, open-mindedness and common
sense.

It is now, perhaps, broadly safe to say that
the exasperating and faintly silly days of
Hollywood hypocrisy and British moral
righteousness have all but disappeared.
Nudity, complete with genitals and pubic
hair, has become commonplace since the

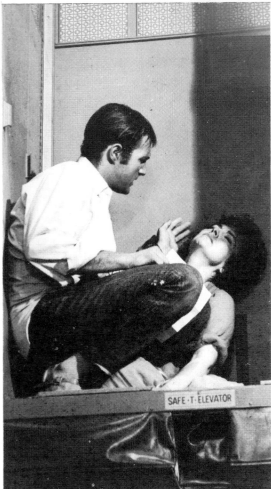

*Above: Kitty
Winn and Al
Pacino in The
Panic in Needle
Park. Left:
James Caan
and Olivia de
Havilland in
Lady in a Cage.
Both films
suffered long
censorship
delays
Opposite:
Stephanie
Beacham and
Marlon Brando
in the
controversial
The
Nightcomers*

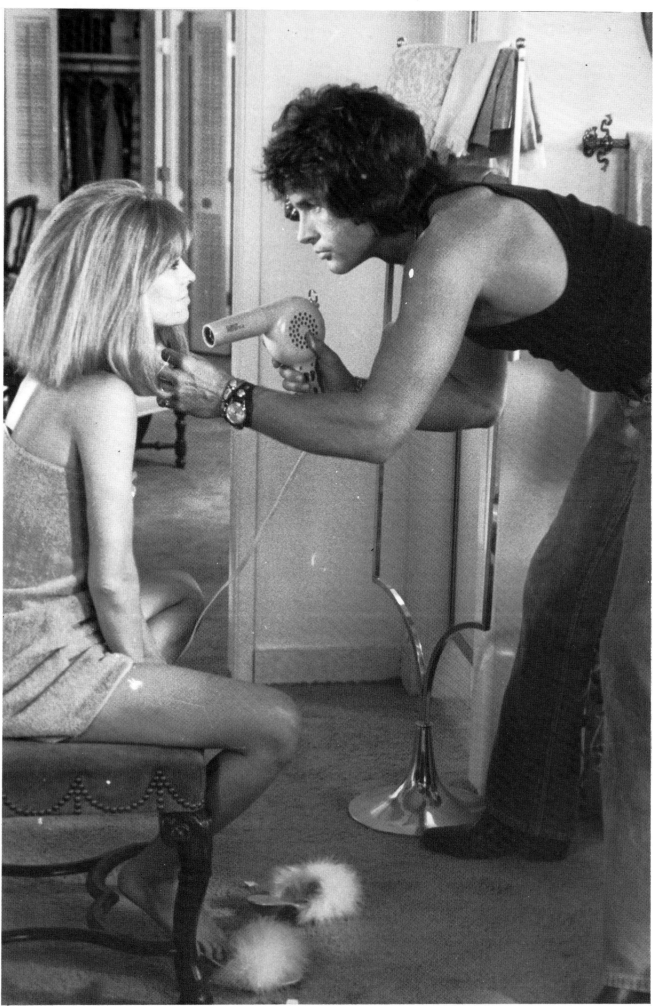

controversial days of *Blow-Up, If . . . . , Hugs and Kisses* and *The Switchboard Operator*. The sex act is now almost a *cliché*. *The Last Detail, Shampoo* and *Alfie Darling* have removed virtually the last language taboos. And even an erection may occasionally be glimpsed, as unblinking watchers of *Flesh, Ain't Misbehavin', WR - Mysteries of the Organism* and *Arabian Nights* may testify. Violence, too, has been largely liberated from the censors' shackles, though with a considerable amount of unease and a great deal of conscience-searching in Britain.

In America, a no-holds-barred situation has been reached in some States, leading to the public showing of the hardest of hard-core pornography, such as *Deep Throat* and *The Devil in Miss Jones*. This has been followed by a curious backlash situation whereby potential prosecutors, frustrated by the lack of obscenity laws relating to film, have successfully sued newspapers carrying notices advertising uncensored films.

In Britain, despite the general liberalisation of attitudes, the survival of formal censorship has so far kept the hard-core pornography at bay, and it is the more ambiguous movies like *Last Tango* and *Emmanuelle* which cause controversy (not to mention *The Language of Love* which, at the time of writing, is the subject of a *sub judice* case) and point up the anomalies of a system which accommodates a trained, largely rational panel of examiners with no statutory teeth on the one hand, and an extraordinary hotch-potch of local-government health committees and what-have-you whose members rarely go to the cinema yet have strong legal powers of censorship on the other.

The BBFC may justifiably be taken to task for giving the thumbs down to such films as *Blow-Out, Immoral Tales, Sweet Movie* and other foreign productions whose reputations suggest that they should be shown, but it has to be remembered that a large part of the Board's responsibility is to the industry which employs it and to gauge public opinion accordingly.

Opposite page: Julie Christie and Warren Beatty in Shampoo — removing virtually the last language taboos

Examples of easily imitatable violence have always concerned the censor. Left: Kung-fu, Headcrusher. Far left: Bruce Lee in Way of the Dragon. Below left: Jack Nicholson joins the bike scene in Hell's Angels on Wheels. Below, far left: ungentlemanly odds against Jody McCrea in The Glory Stompers

Pop go the Movies

Mark Whitman

Like the boy who cried wolf, the musical has tried our patience sorely over the last two decades. Grave warnings brought us rushing to its bedside, only to find the patient sitting up, taking notice and thumbing its nose vigorously at our concern. In the days of its full health and strength, it had been fed on money nurtured by the kind of energetic zest that people like Gene Kelly, Vincente Minnelli or Stanley Donen could bring it. Today both commodities are in alarmingly short supply. Kelly was able to supply the zest in his massive production of *Hello, Dolly!* but a budget in excess of twenty million dollars ruled out of court the likelihood of the film making its money back in an acceptable period of time. The musical has perhaps, after the saddening death throes of *Mame,* passed quietly away at its Hollywood home.

But that is not exactly unexpected. In halcyon days when Rodgers and Hammerstein were every bit as big as Lennon and McCartney, one could confidently expect ballads from the films of *Carousel* and *Oklahoma* to lodge firmly in the Hit Parade. The music and the films caught unerringly the pulse of public taste. Yet the very notion of Lucille Ball's frog-croak of the *Mame* numbers, or even the popular Barbra Streisand's rendering of the livelier songs

from *Hello, Dolly!,* scattering Slade and The Bay City Rollers from the top ten, is risible. A different music has taken over and the fact that this happened twenty years ago is only a token of the cinema's lethargy in facing facts.

The history of pop music in movies — and rock in particular — has been a chequered one. The very year that Deborah Kerr's Victorian governess was teaching Yul Brynner's Siamese monarch to polka in *The King and I,* the kiss-curled Bill Haley erupted on to the screen with *Rock Around the Clock,* a crudely made exploitation quickie that had the commercial good sense to spot the fermentation of a musical revolution.

While middle-aged audiences sighed wistfully at the romantic proprieties of Miss Kerr and Mr Brynner, their offspring were stomping to a different beat and (if we are fully to believe the newspaper reports of the time) rocking in the aisles and tearing cinema seats from the floor. The instant notoriety of rock, the fact that it was branded as decadent and carnal, only enhanced its appeal. Thus separated from their elders, the audience found new totems in the nihilism of Brando's bike-thug from *The Wild One* and in the posthumous cult that mushroomed around James Dean. Amazingly, no bona fide musical was to be forged from this new

Opposite page, as it is and as it was. Top: David Essex as the upcoming pop singer in Stardust. Bottom: Elvis Presley gyrates to the top in Loving You.

57

sound for well over a decade. Even Elvis Presley, most meteoric of the American discoveries, had to satisfy himself with a feeble plot-*cliché* of local-boy-makes-good-as-rock-star in his first musical, *Loving You*. Ironically Presley's best films during the busy '60s were *Kid Galahad* and *Follow That Dream*, movies that minimised his musical abilities and used him more substantially as an actor. It wasn't until the '70s documentaries — *Elvis, That's the Way It Is* and *Elvis On Tour* — that the unconverted had any notion of what dynamism lay in his music and his personal projection of it.

But the criticisms apply equally to the British cinema. The rise (but very rarely fall) of a rock star was the pivot of many uninspired pictures, among them *The Duke Wore Jeans* (Tommy Steele as a character neither so titled nor so attired), *The Golden Disc* (the luckless Terry Dene) and *Idle on Parade* (Anthony Newley, here introduced for the first time to the possibilities of a musical career). Newley and Steele, of course, crossed quickly over to the London Palladium-Las Vegas Establishment, while other personnel of the British pop repertory took care to see that their careers were architected for other forms of survival. Jim

Dale, now a mainstay of The Young Vic, was then compere and guitar-strumming contributor to the television programme "The 6.5 Special" and the film it sired. Adam Faith, now an actor of repute and a musician of some subtlety, was then to be heard hiccoughing listlessly through such epics as *Beat Girl*. Cliff Richard, now the most staid of faimly entertainers, was then sulking menacingly and accusing his vicar of unnatural practices in *Serious Charge*. Mike Sarne, later to become an actor and Hollywood director of *Myra Breckinridge*, was then in the pot with John Leyton and Freddie and the Dreamers in *Every Day's a Holiday*.

To list all the early hybrids conceived in the name of pop music would be too space-consuming. They are, in any case, entertainingly chronicled in "Celluloid Rock" by Philip Jenkinson and Alan Warner (Lorrimer, £1.95). But there were two early pointers of some moment, indications that ultimately the British cinema, even in its dark days, would take a leading role in the presentation of the new musicals.

First came a series of films that recognised that the audiences merely wanted to hear and *see* their record idols — nothing more.

Right: Ringo Starr and Wilfrid Brambell in A Hard Day's Night. Below right: Eleanor Bron and Ringo in Help! Far right: Dave Clark and Barbara Ferris in John Boorman's Catch Us If You Can

They packed as many television-style performances into a film as was humanly possible (the rival medium could never then have afforded so stellar a line-up in one programme) and used only a wisp of a storyline to bind them. Economy with the camera and the cheque book launched many directorial careers, among them Michael Winner's *(Play It Cool)*, Don Sharp's *(It's All Happening)* and Richard Lester's *(It's Trad, Dad)*.

Lester, of course, went on to find a nice surrealist expression of The Beatles' personalities in *A Hard Day's Night* and *Help!* but before then came Canadian director Sidney J Furie's game attempt to make a bona fide musical in *The Young Ones*. The film was anaemic, all the more so in retrospect, and its script crux of youth club members putting on a show would have shamed the B-feature efforts of Mickey Rooney and Judy Garland, but Furie did set out to make a musical *per se*, not just a film in which unintegrated songs were strung artlessly together. But by now its star, Cliff Richard, had mellowed to the softest of pop and the film remained a pleasant enough hybrid. Its successors, *Summer Holiday* and *Wonderful Life*, headed for even safer ground and

Richard's film musical career — through *Finders Keepers* to *Take Me High* — was cursed with unbelievable banality.

A major problem facing anyone seriously interested in making a rock-pop musical at this time was that the necessary groups and artists had had little, if any, dramatic training. Furthermore nobody showed the confidence to commission an original work that would integrate music and narrative instead of imposing the former arbitrarily on the latter. The power and violence of rock made it an unsuitable accompaniment for the kind of happy-ever-after story producers automatically associated with musicals.

A milestone was John Boorman's *Catch Us If You Can* in which the corporate identity of The Dave Clark Five was sunk selflessly into a story of two young people (Clark and Barbara Ferris) trying to escape from the pressures of their urban lives. Apart from marking the debut of an immediately notable director, the film was one of the first to have the courage to use the music of the group as incidental background. Although not a true musical by definition, *Catch Us If You Can* sounded the first acerbic note and, belittled on its release, stands in urgent need of reassessment.

Left: Elvis Presley in Stay Away, Joe. Far left: Paul Jones in Privilege. Below left: Hal Holbrook and Christopher Jones in Wild in the Streets

Paul Nicholas as
the sadistic Cousin
Kevin in Ken
Russell's film of
Tommy, based on
the rock opera by
Pete Townshend
and The Who

Top: David Essex in That'll Be the Day. Centre: Essex and Adam Faith in the sequel, Stardust. Bottom: Slade in Flame

The British film *Privilege* and the American *Wild in the Streets* (released simultaneously in Britain) each spoke of the savagery of rock and the manipulative power of the rock singer. In Peter Watkins' film, Paul Jones was the singer who equates pop and politics, while it was Christopher Jones who took rock right into the White House in a youth-dominated society committed to the extermination of their elders.

Documentary film makers next turned their attention to the burgeoning pop festivals. *Woodstock* (without commentary) communicated an optimism about the peaceful co-existence of armies of young music enthusiasts, but the spirits were dashed by *Gimme Shelter,* the documentary of the Altamont concert by The Rolling Stones at which a man was killed by a force of Hell's Angels. The Beatles staged their own private concert for the benefit of cameras and the fulfilment of their three-picture contract in *Let It Be,* while other public festivals recorded on film included *Monterey Pop, Glastonbury Fayre* and *Wattstax.* Nostalgia edged its way in with *Let the Good Times Roll* where we saw the rock heroes of yesteryear performing, via the split screen process, alongside their younger selves.

Certainly the prevailing mood of nostalgia, the attraction of the '50s, helped the success of an intelligent and resourceful British film, *That'll Be the Day.* The producers took an upcoming pop idol of the '70s, David Essex, and cast him twenty years back in time. This anti-hero, Jim MacLaine, abandons his academic chances and drifts into nihilism before (in the film's final frozen frame) handing over the last of his savings in exchange for a guitar. The background was a relentless barrage of '50s pop, some on record and some played live. Billy Fury played a holiday camp singer and Ringo Starr had a non-singing role as Jim's friend and mentor, Mike.

A sequel was inevitable in so much as that was the way the whole package had been designed. The producers, realising Britain's endemic timidity in matters concerning bona fide film musicals, deliberately set out with *That'll Be the Day* to make a commercial movie that would positively *demand* the sequel they had ready all the while. This was *Stardust,* and it had the unexpected bonus of David Essex's now greatly increased popularity. In the second film, Ray Connolly's script brought Jim up to date (up to the late '60s, at least) via small-time gigs, international stardom, disenchantment and eventual suicide. Adam Faith made a sizeable dramatic contribution as Mike, the sidekick originally created by Ringo Starr, and Paul Nicholas registered strongly as the nose-out-of-joint group member who has to be abandoned on the road to success.

Though infinitely superior to the rise-of-rock-star movies of the late '50s, *Stardust* naturally had the same musical context — musical numbers confined to stage appearances and recording sessions, rather than being integrated in the narrative.

But by this time the theatre had demonstrated the faith that the cinema could never quite muster. There had opened on the London stage three rock musicals that were all enjoying considerable success. David Essex himself had been playing Jesus in "Godspell" (and was expected to appear in the film, *That'll Be the Day* coming as a consolation prize); "Jesus Christ Superstar" was playing to packed houses about one hundred yards away; "Catch My Soul" established a similar following on its transfer to the West End. All owed a debt of conceptual gratitude to the trail-blazing "Hair" but, unlike that technically complex show, these three had immediate movie possibilities.

Godspell was the first to arrive in the cinema, directed by David Greene and with a cast picked from various American companies of the show. Inexplicably, the critics lacerated it for its simplistic naivety (although the stage show had been well received) and the film, arriving in London at the same time as a heatwave, belly-flopped at the box-office. In effect, quite apart from its infectious gaiety, *Godspell* had a great deal to recommend it. Greene and his designer, Brian Eatwell, had gone to a great deal of creative pain to find a mode that was contemporary yet timless enough for their clown-garbed company, enacting the rock Gospel According to Saint Matthew. The use of a deserted New York was vivid. Jesus (Victor Garber) arrives demanding baptism in the Central Park fountain and his enemies are all wrapped up in one smoke-belching monster (borrowed from *The Wizard of Oz*) encountered on the waterfront after a tugboat excursion. Most important of all, the hard-beat, up-tempo music communicates exhilaratingly the sheer joy of being alive. While the theologists could understandably object to a story of Christ without resurrection (the film ends on a shot of the disciples carrying away their crucified master), it remains a major puzzle that audiences were so disinterested in this first bona fide rock musical.

Norman Jewison's *Jesus Christ Superstar* came in with bigger guns blazing and enjoyed a greater initial success, though this was not sustained. Perhaps the success and

Pop concerts on film. Top: part of the vast audience for Woodstock. Centre: The Beatles' recording session in Let It Be. Bottom: Presley makes the long walk to the stage in Elvis – That's the Way It Is

Christ and disciples in Jesus Christ Superstar (right) and Godspell (below)

Right: Lance LeGault's Iago-figure in Catch My Soul, flanked by Tony Joe White and Susan Tyrrell. Opposite: Roger Daltrey as Tommy

celebrity of the stage shows had milked dry the potential audience. Here we had a more petulant Jesus in the flaxen Ted Neeley, but the film was built around the electric Judas of Carl Anderson. Shot in startling Israeli desert locations, the film struggled to capture the attention by deliberate anachronisms, camera tricks and frantic choreography, whereas it was the epic sweep of the music that could (and should) have stood by itself.

Catch My Soul fared little better. The film was assigned to actor-impresario Patrick McGoohan (television's "Danger Man" or, more excitingly, "The Prisoner"). But this same lack of confidence in the music, this grim determination to flood the film with barren stylistics, cooked the goose of this quite literal adaptation of Shakespeare's "Othello." Richie Havens played the black preacher goaded by an Iago-Devil figure (Lance LeGault) into believing his wife guilty of an affair. McGoohan's interpretation was further confused by giving LeGault a warmly human wife (Susan Tyrrell, contributing the film's best-rounded performance) but installing him in a sinister black mobile home that pointed up the demonic and supernatural aspect of the character.

But naturalism hadn't helped the rock musical and, discouraged by the comparative disappointments of these three films, it rested a while and inevitably mutated. In the interim a new young director, Richard Loncraine, breathed fire into the old pop-group-makes-good plot in *Flame,* a showcase for the talents of Slade, a group with a sub-Beatles kind of quirky humour and tonsil-baring brio. A keenly cynical script (and one superb performance from Tom Conti as the group's ultra-sophisticated wheeler-dealer promoter) made this one of the best films of its kind.

During the gestation period Apple, The Beatles' own company, had backed a rock musical entitled *Son of Dracula* (which had the working title of *Count Downe*), but the film became legally ensnared in inter-company tangles and was never shown publicly in Britain. A soundtrack album escaped, complete with patches of dialogue, to suggest a lively sense of fun. Harry Nilsson was the vampire opting for mortality in order to love Suzanna Leigh; Ringo Starr was the time-tripping Merlin, Dracula's perpetual adviser. In the light of the extravagances that have followed, one wonders if Apple might be well advised to sample the market now.

There was equal irreverence in Brian De Palma's energetic *Phantom of the Paradise*

which purported (for simplicity of description) to be a rock version of *Phantom of the Opera*, but was in fact a satirical fusion of elements of "Faust," "Frankenstein" and "The Picture of Dorian Gray". Paul Williams (who also composed the top-notch score) played Swan, the ever-youthful head of Death Records, pledged to contract new souls for his satanic master. Meanwhile Swan's earthly instincts are to pirate a cantata written by Winslow Leach (William Finley) and use it as the music to open The Paradise, his twenty-four-hour rock palace. The vengeful Leach gets his head crushed in a record-pressing machine and lives on, a voiceless disfiguration, to haunt The Paradise and supervise the career of an adored girl singer. This last part is true enough to the Claude Rains phantom, but the climactic orgy of coast-to-coast televised massacre, as Leach brings a final revenge to free his soul, is pure De Palma. This extraordinary, original piece of film-making deserves to be seen and is in many respects superior to Ken Russell's *Tommy*, the film that eclipsed it on its first release.

Tommy springs from a rock opera written by Pete Townshend and The Who. It had only been performed live and on record before Russell opted to film it. (A stage production has subsequently been mounted.) It fell to Russell to find a look, a style for the screen *Tommy* and it fell to The Who to link together their various songs so that the narrative remains a true opera. Given such casting as Oliver Reed (Tommy's stepfather) and Jack Nicholson (The Harley Street specialist) the sound track has a certain curiosity value.

Roger Daltrey, most charismatic of modern rock singers, was a natural choice for the title role (and went on to work again for Russell in *Lisztomania,* a loose biography that sees the composer as the Mick Jagger of his day) and Daltrey manages movingly well to convey the silent torture of the young Tommy, shocked into a near vegetable-like stage of deafness, dumbness and blindness after seeing his father killed.

His final liberation, his rise and fall as a pinball wizard and then as a marketable messiah, gives Russell scope (perhaps a little too much scope) for striking out at all the sacred cows. The director claimed before shooting started that "Tommy" was the only post-war musical work that actually communicated to young people, and he certainly made a vibrant and stimulating film that, opening within a week of *Funny Lady* and at an adjacent cinema, proved just where the musical was at in the '70s.

The Rocky Horror Picture Show, the first post-*Tommy* rock musical, had a pedigree dating back to days in experimental theatre. Just as "Hair" had opened off-Broadway and finally taken the street by storm to become an international success, first with the blue jeans and then the blue rinses, so "The Rocky Horror Show" moved from experiment to Establishment. The film, directed by Jim Sharman (the original stage director), is loaded with movie references that are quite sophisticated in concept, if a trifle clumsy in execution. The *cliché* of the sciene fiction double-feature programme is mercilessly guyed and the case-history of the couple (Barry Bostwick and Susan Sarandon) who stumble upon the strange mansion of monster-maker Frank N Furter is set within the framework of an Edgar Lustgarten crime thriller, the criminologist himself being played by Charles Gray.

But, despite the Frankenstein-Dracula overtones, Tim Curry's character is "just a sweet transvestite from transexual Transylvania," a galactic emissary passing the time by making creatures for his/her own sexual gratification. The score (writer-composer-lyricist Richard O'Brien also appears in the film) is poundingly good and the audience has by now learned what to ask and what to expect of such a film.

With no other genre has what is pop (or popular) taken so long to take over. If any form of drama — be it war, western or contemporary — had clung for twenty years to outmoded social notions, it could never reasonably have hoped to survive. Yet the musical persisted in lavishing vast sums of money on outdated concepts twenty years after the weekly statistics of the Top Ten had given the lie to public taste.

Most likely it is not to everyone's taste, but pop art continues to thrive in the movie musical. Pete Walker, a prodigious sexploitation entrepreneur, has turned his canny attention to a rock version of George du Maurier's *Trilby,* the Svengali story, and, at the time of writing, Barbra Streisand and boy-friend Jon Peters continue to woo Elvis Presley with offers to do a rock re-make of *A Star Is Born,* filmed twice already — with Janet Gaynor and Fredric March, then Judy Garland and James Mason.

The stage musical successes of the moment are either difficult ("Applause") or expensive ("A Little Night Music") to film, or have already appeared on celluloid ("Gypsy" and "Billy"). The theatre, in any case, is more middle-class in its pretensions. For moviegoers, young or old, it is to the pop musical one must now look for the rude vigour and raw energy that are prerequisites of the genre.

Opposite: film influences in rock opera. Top: Tim Curry in The Rocky Horror Picture Show. Bottom: William Finley in Phantom of the Paradise

Rectangle into Square

Adrian Turner

Film-going is essentially a community experience, but it is also an activity which verges on the clandestine. A few hundred people (they used to be numbered in thousands) allow themselves to be ushered into a cavernous room — resembling anything from an air terminal to a Byzantine cathedral — and be plunged into virtual darkness.

You may find yourself seated next to a total stranger for three hours or more yet, when the lights are down and the curtains have been swept dramatically aside, your attention is directed solely towards the illuminated rectangle. It is a wonderful moment when the house-lights fade and the curtains open: the chatter of the audience dwindles away in anticipation, the pencil-thin beams from the usherettes' torches dart around in a final search for empty seats and the picture show is running at last.

Some way behind and above the heads of the crowd, two rods of carbon or a terrifyingly powerful xenon lamp produce an intense light which reflects on to a mirror; it passes through a minutely proportioned gate, then through the film itself which is travelling vertically at ninety feet per minute, through an exactly ground lens, through the final barrier of sound-proofing glass and out into black space,

winging across the auditorium until its career is halted by the waiting screen.

The subtle variations of light and shade and the combinations of colours magnified a thousand times produce a cohesive image which reflects back towards the people. Each and every individual receives the picture and sound (which has arrived by an altogether different route) and the individual response mingles with the rest to produce the community experience that so distinguishes the cinema.

Of course, not every cinema is as luxurious as the Empire Leicester Square, nor as technically sophisticated as the Odeon Marble Arch, nor as rarified as the Academy, nor as conscious of heritage as the National Film Theatre. Indeed, cinemas can be rather unpleasant places to visit — cold and drafty, unfriendly and almost derelict, and in these days of multi-units, uncomfortably claustrophobic. There may be no rake to the stalls floor which will make the reading of subtitles from behind a tall gentleman an enterprise requiring guile and patience, not to mention supple neck muscles. Your neighbour may be channelling cigarette smoke into your eyes; the audience may be noisily grappling with sweet wrappers, pelting the screen with popcorn or consuming pungent hot-dogs; an old man

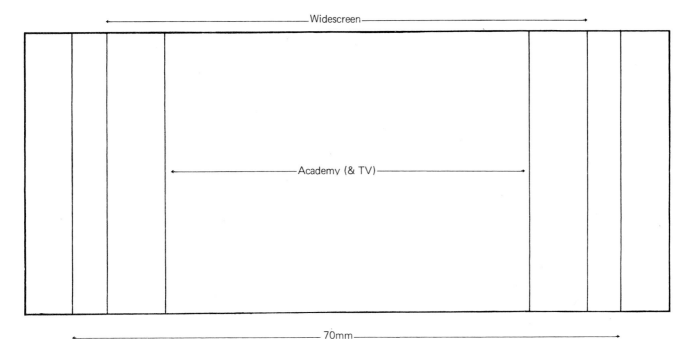

Academy (& TV)

70mm

CinemaScope

The various ratios most common in modern film making

may be snoring in the row behind and the couple in front may insist on a running commentary. Very few cinemas offer perfect conditions – or, indeed, audiences.

But the shortcomings of the majority are, I suggest, infinitely preferable to watching films on television. Even if you have a struggle seeing every square-inch of the screen or are subjected to one or all of these sundry annoyances, a group of strangers sitting in the dark and responding in unison constitutes the life-essence of the cinema. This special atmosphere cannot be simulated on television, and when you see a good film in a cinema it will probably seem terrible on TV.

Conversely, a bad film in a cinema might improve on TV. As a rule the films of good directors suffer disastrously from televising while the films of indifferent directors improve. This is because a good director knows his medium inside-out and exploits it to the full – visually, aesthetically and intellectually. Lesser men do not (which is why they are second grade) and their films suffer less from the miniaturisation and the unceremoniousness of TV viewing.

Distractions at home are many and varied, just as in a cinema, but the lack of a screen that dominates the room serves to accentuate the domestic disruptions. The kettle may be whistling, the dog may be barking to be let out, the traffic outside may be hooting loudly and your viewing partners may be chatting or pressing to switch channels for "Match of the Day", "Omnibus" or even another movie.

While the cinema audience is largely a captive one, and the various distractions are at least related to the cinema, the TV viewer is subjected to diversions which are unrelated to the film. Even the two modes of viewing encourage two distinctive definitions: you "watch" a film on television, underlining the more casual approach to viewing, while you "see" a film in a cinema, emphasising the more serious commitment you make when you actually go out and buy a ticket.

The dedicated film-buff can make certain he is alone, or with sympathetic company, when he watches a film on television (I know some who disconnect their telephones, surround themselves with food and coffee and stick a "back in ninety-seven minutes" notice on their front doors) but he needs the company of strangers if he is to enjoy the film fully. The responses of other people are essential, especially with comedies.

Watching, say, any of the Marx Brothers' films, Billy Wilder's *Some Like it Hot,* an Ealing comedy such as *Kind Hearts and Coronets* or Mel Brooks' *The Producers* is a totally different experience to seeing them in a cinema. You can savour every one of Groucho's wisecracks or Marilyn Monroe's conversation-stoppers without an audience drowning them in laughter left over from the previous joke, to be sure, but this is like watching comedy from out in the street. You need to get close to the action, which the sharp contrast on a TV screen prevents. The generated response of an audience you experience in a cinema contributes enormously to your evaluation and enjoyment of a film; laughter is an infectious thing and there is nothing so alienating as hearing your own laughter echoing around your room. This is why so many films, and not only comedies, seem curiously and distressingly stale when you watch them again a few years later on TV. Your original

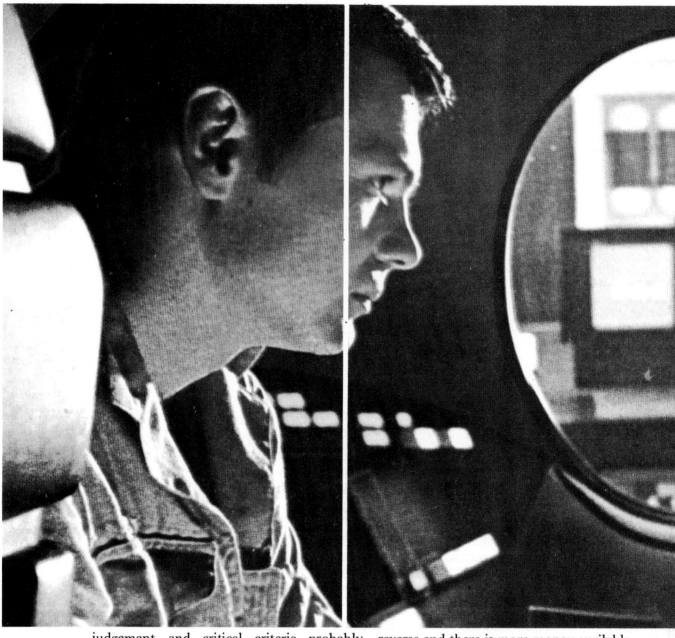

judgement and critical criteria probably haven't changed much, *but your viewing environment has.*

Some Like it Hot is one of my favourite comedies but I hardly laughed at all when I watched it on TV a few years ago. Worried that I had somehow gone off the film, I went to see it shortly after in a cinema. The film was its own brilliantly comic self. I was part of a large and very appreciative audience who were living with the film. Television, however, is the cinema's grave-yard, the place where movies go to die in droves.

TV is essentially a medium for information and discussion, providing instant news and capable of reflecting the times in which we live better than films since it's so quick. All you need is a 16mm camera and a sound crew and your report can be broadcast that night, even if it was filmed in Los Angeles or Hong Kong. But most films are better at drama than TV. The time factor works in

reverse and there is more money available.

Films have taken over British television because they're comparatively cheap and require no imagination from TV workers. During the 1974-5 Christmas period over forty feature films were broadcast on the three networks and not one of them came in the top five of the JICTAR Ratings (printed in "Cinema-TV Today," 18 January 1975), not even David Lean's *The Bridge on the River Kwai* for which the BBC had paid an exceptional (but not unreasonable) £120,000. Amazingly, the highest rated film over Christmas with an estimated 6.5 million viewers was *The Most Dangerous Man in the World.* Also amazingly, the highest rated programme was the final of Magnus Magnusson's egg-head quiz "Mastermind," which must have cost the BBC a fraction of what they paid for *Kwai.*

While a few new films become financial blockbusters and keep the commercial cinema in business, television has killed off

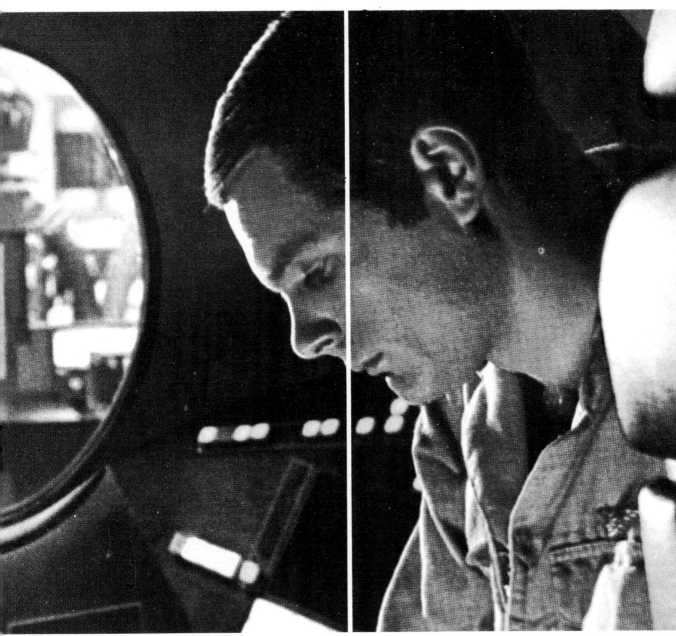

the cinema's history; as the Christmas ratings showed decisively, feature films are not very popular with TV viewers, but distributors invariably withdraw a film after it has been televised and exhibitors shy away from showing those which are still commercially available. In so doing they are keeping old films away from where they belong, in cinemas, and in many instances they are turning their backs on a healthy profit. A television screening can often stimulate or revive interest in a film if it is shown after a judicious interval.

But not all films suffer disastrously from being shown on television. My favourite film is undoubtedly Stanley Kubrick's *Dr Strangelove,* which I have seen twice on TV and over ten times in cinemas. Kubrick's razor-sharp nuclear war comedy loses all dramatic impetus on TV, especially if it's shown on the commercial channel where the breaks for advertisements destroy any film's structure. Kubrick's brilliantly conceived technique of constantly changing locations, each with its own distinctive visual style, is destroyed by the insensitive and bland texture of the cathode-ray tube.

Sidney Lumet's *Fail Safe,* however, comes across tolerably well on TV. Lumet's nuclear war film is played straight (and is, incidentally, far less effective than Kubrick's film since nuclear war is too appalling a concept to take seriously) and takes place for most of the time in a single room with the President (Henry Fonda) hanging on to a telephone. Whereas Kubrick's masterpiece is triumphantly filmic, Lumet's film is static and wilfully claustrophobic. Movies which don't move are less vulnerable to the cancellation ethic of television because they're more like TV programmes, a bit stagey and cramped.

It's not merely a question of form versus content (*Dr Stangelove* is very wordy, but it's also very funny) but a question of approach and aesthetics. Lumet's *Twelve*

Angry Men is another film which loses nothing in dramatic tension on television since most of the action is confined to a single jury-room. Mike Nichols' *Who's Afraid of Virginia Woolf?* is another chamber work, transferred *in toto* from the stage production, which emerges unscathed due to the claustrophobic setting and the strident performances from the small cast. Films that are intellectual word-games function in the same way as TV plays, but when a director as good as, say, Kubrick or Joseph Losey *(The Servant, Accident)* make a film in which form and content are inextricably fused, the small screen seriously undermines the intention.

Alfred Hitchcock is often referred to as Hollywood's "supreme technician" and while one of his marginal works, *Dial M for Murder,* functions as a made-for-TV movie (the kind of hybrid that David Quinlan writes about elsewhere in this book), the similarly plotted *Strangers on a Train* loses most of its tension because it moves at a whirlwind pace. Because the TV viewer's eye has to absorb extraneous objects, like a vase of flowers, a bookcase or a French window, the small screen is unable to cope with the pace since everything is much smaller and the eye has less time to assimilate detail.

A case could be made that horror films are more frightening at home because the cinema audience acts as a kind of tranquilliser. I don't very much care for horror films but there is certainly something scary about watching, say, *The Devil Rides Out* or *Them!* alone in your house late at night, especially if the wind suddenly opens your living-room door like a spook. I can think of no other genre where the arguments roughly balance out, but Hitchcock's *Psycho* (surely the greatest horror movie ever) was made specifically for a group of strangers sitting in the dark. *Psycho* is moderately effective on television but when that car suddenly refuses to sink into the swamp behind the Bates Motel the shocked silence of an audience outweighs the response of the TV viewer in atmosphere. And when the car finally sinks into the morass with a sickening gurgle you can physically feel the cinema audience change its allegiance to Anthony Perkins.

You sweat at home, to be sure, but it's not quite the same thing as smelling the sweat (and the hot-dogs) of other people. Hitchcock knows instinctively how to use camera and montage to create suspense and *Psycho*, for much of the time, is a wordless movie. Along with John Ford, Howard Hawks, Orson Welles and a few others, Hitchcock's films are pure cinema and all but his more pedestrian efforts (such as the

quickly made *Dial M For Murder*) inevitably lose much of their impact when shown on TV. Hitchcock is a great showman; he knows how to manipulate an audience, but without that audience his films become objects for cool-headed analysis: perfect for the scholar or critic researching a thesis, but not for emotional participation.

I have just mentioned pace and television's inability to keep up with it. The televising of subtitled films accentuates this handicap to an intolerable degree. To take just one example: in the first six months of 1975 three films were premiered on TV before they opened in London. These were Peter Hall's *Akenfield* (of which more later), Philippe Mora's Depression document *Brother, Can You Spare A Dime?* and Alain Resnais's *Stavisky*. I watched *Stavisky* in colour on BBC-2 for just long enough to see that I would like it (this took around forty-five minutes) and then switched over to BBC-1 to catch the tail-end of an interview with David Hockney (and how's that for idiotic programme planning?). Resnais's style is renowned for its elliptical cutting, its flashback and flashforward techniques and dislocated time structure; his films move extremely quickly and make considerable intellectual demands on an audience.

My French is far from fluent though I probably rely too heavily on subtitles. *Stavisky* is not by any means an extreme case (indeed, it's Resnais's most accessible film to date) but I found that by the time I had lowered my eyes to read a line of dialogue the scene had changed. One was constantly endeavouring to keep abreast of both subtitles and images with the inevitable result that a clear understanding of neither emerged. In a cinema the screen dominates the line of vision and after a few minutes the eye absorbs the titles and pictures as a single image. Because a TV screen often represents an area of less than 1 per cent of a cinema screen, the subtitles become correspondingly smaller and less easy to read. In addition to this, the technical process of televising films can render the subtitles in a darker shade which adds yet another obstacle to appreciation and enjoyment.

So far I have confined the argument to films made in the Academy ratio or the now normally accepted wide-screen ratio. I have deliberately avoided extra-wide or epic-scale films in order to define why films look bad on television without resorting immediately to an argument which depends on dimensions and aspect ratios. But I can hold it off no longer and must now consider films made in a 35mm 'Scope process (such as Panavision, Techniscope and CinemaScope), a 70mm process or even Cinerama.

Before progressing with some illustrations it should be noted that a television screen has a fixed aspect ratio of 1.33:1, that is, a screen roughly a third wider than it is high. This is the ratio known as Academy which was used for all sound films until the early '50s when wide-screen became available, using an aspect ratio varying between 1.66:1 to 1.85:1.

Even so, some directors prefer to use the Academy ratio to this day (Losey's *The Go-Between*, for example) and most Continental films are shot on Academy.

'Scope films are generally 2.35:1, though the original CinemaScope productions (the first was *The Robe* in 1953) had magnetic soundtracks with an aspect ratio of 2.55:1. 70mm films require a screen with a ratio of 2:1. Although a large screen is ideal, physical dimensions are unimportant: it is the relationship between width and height that is the key factor. As you can see, all but Academy films lose something when shown on television and when ITV broadcast *The Robe* early in 1975 viewers were denied approximately half of the frame area.

When television first began transmitting feature films there was no problem of cropping since everything that was available was made in the Academy ratio. 'Scope films are more numerous on TV nowadays since the special equipment became cheaper and more versatile during the '60s and the TV companies now have access to films made before 1971, assuming that the "gentleman's agreement" of a five-year delay is honoured.

Perhaps due to reasons shortly to be discussed, film-makers are electing to shoot in the normal wide-screen ratio or even Academy: Fred Zinnemann's *The Day of the Jackal*, John Schlesinger's *The Day of the Locust*, Francis Ford Coppola's *The Godfather* and Norman Jewison's *Rollerball* would almost certainly have been made in 'Scope or even 70mm ten years ago. Now they are made in wide-screen with an aesthetic eye to eventual showing on TV. Directors know that their efforts will be ruined on TV (as many have regretted to me) but they would prefer viewers to see as much of their work as possible.

A notable exception to this is Peter Hall's film of *Akenfield*, which was financed by London Weekend Television and shown on TV and premiered at the Paris Pullman Cinema simultaneously. Peter Hall made the film in Techniscope so as to capture the extreme flatness of the Suffolk landscape and to underline the villagers' subordination to the land that dominates and destroys their lives. Like John Schlesinger's fine adaptation of Thomas Hardy's *Far From the Madding Crowd*, a 70mm film which has been shown twice on television, Hall's film constantly showed the country-folk dwarfed physically and spiritually by the harsh beauty of the countryside. Consequently, much of Hall's message passed by unseen by the large TV audience. The entire opening sequence, for example, consisted of shots of the hero walking along country lanes and greeting neighbours — but he was often out of sight. *Akenfield* is a supremely cinematic work but it was, incredibly, considered to be a television production which also happened to be shown in cinemas. Even "The Times" allocated the film to their television critic and not their film critic.

It is now customary for the credit titles of 'Scope or 70mm films to be shown either squeezed laterally (the ITV method) or shown in the correct ratio with a dark band running above and below (the BBC method). Both networks then show the main body of the film on the 1.33:1 ratio. Television projectors, which are called Telecine machines, can "scan" the wide frame area but an embarrassing problem of space arises should two characters conduct a conversation from opposing edges. This scanning technique, though fully rehearsed beforehand, adds camera "movements" to a film which were not intended and seriously undermines the overall style of a film. Indeed, directors like John Ford and David Lean often hold their cameras perfectly still to achieve a dramatic effect.

Then there is the question of selection. A

conversation between two actors does not necessarily mean that the actor who is speaking is the most important; the reactions of the listener may be crucial, yet the Telecine operator faced with a problem of space (either he does nothing and we see only a piece of desert or a table, or he "pans" across to one actor) will invariably concentrate on the actor who does the most talking. And when a great many people are talking or there is a crowd scene the whole system falls apart at the seams. The logical extension to this would be a bar on 'Scope films ever appearing on TV or an agreement that such films are shown in the correct ratio. But then, of course, the screen would be further reduced in size which would increase the viewer's vulnerability to distraction and eye-strain.

The 70mm and Cinerama films are more recent and tend to feature big stars, big stories and big everything. Although ITV televised Stanley Kubrick's *Spartacus* in a longer version than was shown in cinemas you could justifiably complain that you only saw half the film width-wise. This type of film (*Lawrence of Arabia*, *West Side Story*, *Barabbas* and *El Cid* are others) are publicised for their spectacular qualities: their elaborate battles, their vivid dance routines and arena sequences. But on the small TV screen these scenes (which supposedly attract the viewers) are totally ineffective due to the lack of size and the thin sound reproduction.

At least half the sight-gags in Stanley Kramer's *It's a Mad, Mad, Mad, Mad World* were missing on television and the film was consequently only half as funny. Anthony Mann's magnificent *El Cid* is one of the very few blockbusters which can be called Epic, yet its tapestry-like surface and its superbly choreographed battle scenes were appallingly compressed and the famous tournament scene lost all of its hoof-pounding splendour. *Grand Prix,* a large-scale racing drama directed in Cinerama by John Frankenheimer, contained some astonishing montage sequences and split-screen effects which were utterly destroyed on the TV screen. Perhaps most ludicrous of all was the TV showing of *How the West was Won,* a spectacular if basically empty survey of the roots of modern America. Filmed in the original three-screen Cinerama, the BBC transmitted a 35mm reduction print with the two dividing lines still visible. But these two blurred and brown lines, an embarrassing hang-over from the original Cinerama combined negative, were at the extreme edges of the TV screen; action on either side, and there was plenty, was non-existent.

Although smaller films suffer less, the effect remains acutely damaging. The famous climactic cattle drive in Howard Hawks's *Red River* (shot in black and white in the Academy ratio) or the marvellous feeling of spaciousness in John Ford's poetic westerns are reduced to nothingness. And yet these scenes made the films what they are, what made them famous and what made the group of strangers sitting in the dark respond to in unison. Given all the distractions — the lack of sound and size (and sometimes colour), the breaks for news bulletins and commercials and the frequent cutting by ITV of scenes — everything in films, from acting to art direction, from narrative to subtitling, from music scores to rhythmic editing, suffers from showing on television.

We have taken many detours to arrive at this conclusion so perhaps, finally, some qualification is necessary. This article was written in London where I live; indeed, it was actually written in a cinema building within earshot of a film that has been televised many times. London is lucky to have a few cinemas where you can see old

Christ (Max Von Sydow) and the six and a half disciples that a television screen could accommodate. George Stevens' The Greatest Story Ever Told

films which have been shown on TV. Cinemas such as the National Film Theatre, the Everyman Hampstead, the Electric and Starlight Clubs are keeping alive the heritage of the cinema. People living outside London are forced to watch old films on television since the circuit cinemas and provincial independents will rarely risk showing a film that has been televised. So while my argument might gain aesthetic approval from readers, the brutal facts of life may weigh heavily against. It's all very well leading a cloistered life in London but it's a different matter if you happen to live in Carlisle or Wells.

The televising of feature films undoubtedly stimulates interest among the community — the cult for Humphrey Bogart, for example, would surely not be as intense were it not for frequent TV exposure — but there is a complete lack of back-up support and encouragement from Wardour Street. While this article has attempted to resist the temptation to discuss the various economic factors involved and reveal the despicable practice of "junking" prints which few people seem to be aware of, I strongly believe that it is due to laziness and sheer apathy from within certain offices in Wardour Street that the situation has been allowed to get to its present unsatisfactory level. If Wardour Street had the energy and the interest or some younger blood to replace the old men who still operate along outdated '50s lines, they would be less eager to send their "product" to the TV grave-yard. They could revive massive interest in the cinema and nourish what is already there.

"If I could choose a film which would justify the existence of Hollywood", wrote Robin Wood in 1968, "it would be *Rio Bravo*." Howard Hawks' masterpiece was revived in France and Italy a couple of years ago and was a tremendous success. This was mainly due to the French and Italian governments' policy to restrict by law the number of hours available to TV networks for the transmission of cinema films. In Britain, *Rio Bravo* has been killed off by repeated screenings on television and there are now no prints available for cinemas. But like the man said at the end of Billy Wilder's *Irma La Douce:* "That's another story."

Faces that Fit

Susan d'Arcy

What makes a star? Why is stardom such an ephemeral quality, so difficult to define but so easy to recognise? "To describe it is like trying to catch a moonbeam in a bottle," says veteran director Vincente Minnelli. He not only moulded the careers of any number of stars, he married one (July Garland) and fathered another (Liza Minnelli).

Alexander Walker observed in his book "Stardom": "The studio system was a harsh regime: a form of 20th century slavery. But like earlier systems of servitude, those whom it did not destroy were preserved by it for marvellous spans of time."

Today there is no vast publicity machine building stars, fanning the public interest, feeding the demand for information. At best, today, information is sketchy. Behind all the current superstars — Robert Redford, James Caan, Jack Nicholson, Burt Reynolds — there is a decade of hard graft, indifferent roles. The necessity of learning the craft.

"Stardom, talent, is a natural gift some people have," says director Norman Jewison. "It's difficult to pinpoint. As far as stars go vulnerability is important and definitely sex appeal. We're all looking for a lover, for a father image, for something. There are certain people who supply that for us. Most film stars have that. The camera is a strange instrument. Sometimes you don't have to do

much — you look through the camera and you can see it."

The quality that the camera loves is an extraordinary thing, and the actor most transformed by the lens is surely William Atherton, the central character in John Schlesinger's *The Day of the Locust* and one of the stars of *The Hindenburg*. "He has enormous charisma on the screen, more so than in real life I think," says John Schlesinger. "Since the character was an observer it was necessary to have someone who seemed to have a lot going on inside and there are a limited number of actors who can suggest that. There was something interesting in his hostility and nervousness, sensitivity, rawness, a questioning kind of personality that intrigued me.

"That quality has nothing to do with stardom at all because stardom simply means charisma on the screen and that you can't take your eyes off them. That's a quality that doesn't depend on inner life."

Atherton was previously in Steven Spielberg's *The Sugarland Express* and had two cameo performances prior to that, *Class of '44* and *Precinct 45 — Los Angeles Police.* In real life Atherton is a sincere, amiable and honest man but only passingly reminiscent of the charismatic character in *The Day of the Locust.* But he was clearly

*Opposite:
Cybill
Shepherd in
At Long Last
Love*

77

marked for stardom because, quite simply, the camera transformed him.

He gained his experience on the New York stage, working in experimental theatre and earning a reputation for appearing in material by successful new playrights. Atherton's very difference from his screen self works for him rather than against him. Unlike many rising talents he is seldom recognised, and is allowed to maintain his private identity. "I have a theory that you are only recognised when you want to be recognised," he says. His striving is less for success than to be good. His fervent belief in the philosophy of Aesthetic Realism has enabled him to join in the race but remain distanced from it.

It was easier for an actor to become a star under the studio system. Everything dictated

Fast-rising actresses Valerie Perrine (left) and Deborah Raffin (right). Opposite: William Atherton in The Day of the Locust

the ultimate success: publicity was geared towards it, stories were developed by the studio to house and exploit the embryo talent. Now the individual has to create his own whirlwinds to get ahead.

Possibly the luckiest actor in the early '70s was Jon Finch. He had the face, the presence, the aura of stardom and the good fortune to make three major films on the trot (Polanski's *Macbeth*, Hitchcock's *Frenzy*, Robert Bolt's *Lady Caroline Lamb*). At that time few established stars had three films going. But for Jon Finch the light burned bright and was extinguished even faster. A couple of projects failed to materialise, one indifferent film did (*The Final Programme*). The moment had passed.

"I think actors are pretty courageous people," says director Arthur Penn. "They

deal out in the open with private feelings that most of us don't like to have excused. And that's pretty gutsy, I think. The ones with the ability to really deliver that emotion again and again are also pretty remarkable artists."

One such is surely Valerie Perrine, the ravishing honey blonde with the high-pitched little-girl voice and the spectacular body. Her life story reads like a more creative achievement of the fiction department at a Hollywood studio. Miss Perrine spent two years dancing in a topless show at Las Vegas before being discovered by George Roy Hill and cast as the exotic Montana Wildhack in *Slaughterhouse-Five*. Her second film was *The Last American Hero* and her third, *Lenny*, won her the Best Actress award at the Cannes Film Festival, an Oscar

nomination and finally, a belief in herself as an actress and the fierce desire to continue acting. Her new film, *W.C. Fields and Me* with Rod Steiger directed by Arthur Hiller, makes continued success inevitable.

What separates Valerie Perrine from many other new actresses is her frank enjoyment of stardom, the way she relishes the full treatment and honestly demands the bounty a successful career automatically brings. "You mustn't believe all this too much," she says gesturing to the luxurious suite she joyously occupies. "At home I'm the same old slob I always was."

Slob, by her own definition, she may be, but it doesn't intrude on the stardom she has earned. In the less concerned days of the '70s the lines between the public and private persona have all but vanished. The days

Susan Sarandon in The Great Waldo Pepper. She has also starred in The Front Page and The Rocky Horror Picture Show

80

when Joan Crawford was a star twenty-four hours a day have long gone and the woman in the supermarket next to you is just as likely to be an off-duty superstar as a housewife.

Beautiful, ethereal Deborah Raffin, chosen by Gregory Peck for the female lead in *The Dove* for her "Grace Kelly quality of stillness" has every chance of becoming a star. Her first film was *40 Carats*, then came *The Dove*, and from that she went into a starring role in *Once Is Not Enough*, based on the best-selling novel by Jacqueline Susann. Deborah maintains a firm stand against nudity on celluloid and has so far managed to avoid stripping off. She has even turned down three good offers (where she admits the nudity was central to the story) because they called for baring all. On *Once is Not*

Enough she resisted the repeated attempts and even ran the risk of losing the part (other actresses were tested after she refused to do the nude scenes). Eventually the producers returned to her but the persuasion continued, although it was unsuccessful.

Whether or not Deborah Raffin has staying power remains to be seen. She admits that she acts for fun, not for financial security, and her marriage and possibly future motherhood would always come before her career. This attitude may possibly make for happiness, but it is less certain to result in continued stardom where hunger is a healthy prerequisite.

If Miss Raffin is currently being launched and promoted as a potential star, that is vastly different to the sudden spark when an actor "happens" in a film. Such an actor is

Richard Dreyfuss who erupted in *The Apprenticeship of Duddy Kravitz* – all twitching, nervous energy, snapping fingers and aggression. The kind of star presence he possessed in that film made you wonder why you hadn't really been aware of him as the one who got away in *American Graffiti*. His new film, *Jaws*, is based on the gigantic best-seller. Since then Dreyfuss has made a film in England called *Inserts*. Above all he is a nonconformist. Even at this early stage in his career he has decided he dislikes the interview and resists as many as possible. Whether he can afford this bravado, time alone will illustrate. Many would argue that at no stage in a career can an actor afford to disregard publicity because it is a denial of the very ingredient which makes for success: public interest.

Stardom, as Alexander Walker pointed out, is very much a Hollywood phenomenon. It happens less frequently to British actors. One British actor who should have become a star in recent years is Edward Fox. For years he was in the shadow of his younger brother, James, but then came Fred Zinnemann and a best-selling novel "The Day of the Jackal" by Frederick Forsyth. The build-up was spectacular: "Edward Fox is the Jackal" shrieked the banners. "How Edward Fox became the Jackal" proclaimed the headlines. But while the film happened in a big way, Edward Fox, an accomplished actor and genial man, didn't.

Very often in the '70s, it seems, the film is bigger than the sum of its parts, including the actors. Malcolm McDowell is a case in point. He has starred in three of the most extraordinary films of the last decade: *If....*, *A Clockwork Orange* and *O Lucky Man!* He resists the idea of superstardom. When *Time* magazine called him a superstar after *A Clockwork Orange* he thought it ludicrous. "How can you call somebody who's only made five films a superstar? What is it anyway? Mind you, I was thrilled when I read it, because Time don't use superlatives all that often, but I didn't keep rushing to the loo to read it secretly." Although he has continued working, both in films (*Royal Flash*) and theatre ("Entertaining Mr Sloane"), Malcolm McDowell has not lost his anonymity because most of the public went to see those three remarkable films for the films themselves, or perhaps for the directors, but arguably less for the actors in them.

Stars are seldom a product of the big disaster films — or before that, epics — most of which boast large international casts of established actors. An exception was *Nicholas and Alexandra* which charted the downfall of Czarist Russia. A cast of largely

Left: Richard Dreyfuss in The Apprenticeship of Duddy Kravitz

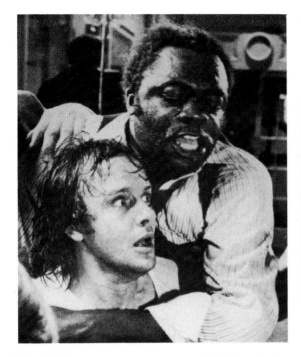

British theatre actors were assembled in Spain led by Michael Jayston and Janet Suzman in the title roles and Tom Baker as Rasputin. In spite of the money and care lavished on it and the publicity which attended it, none of these three achieved cinema stardom as a result, although all continue to work prolifically and Miss Suzman is acknowledged as one of the finest actresses in the British theatre and has latterly achieved considerable success on television. Another big British film which failed to make a star of its leading man was *Young Winston* which launched the career of a likeable young actor, Simon Ward. Another successful theatre actor, he gave an admirable performance as the young Winston Churchill in Richard Attenborough's sensitive and moving film, but since then his films generally have failed to reach large audiences.

This failure of a big film to promote stardom seems more an English weakness than an American one. *The Godfather* gave a boost to the careers of Al Pacino and James Caan and provided the watershed for their later success. *The Godfather Part II* should work the same trick for Robert DeNiro who played the young Vito Corleone. DeNiro has, in fact, been around for some time and owes some credit for his success to director Martin Scorsese for whom he made *Mean Streets.* DeNiro is better known in America where *Mean Streets* was more widely seen and his other pre-Godfather film, *Hang the Drum Slowly* became a cult success. DeNiro stars in Scorsese's subsequent films, *Taxi Driver* and *Raging Bull. Taxi Driver* in fact boasts a fascinating line-up: in addition to De Niro there are Harvey Keitel (featured in Scorsese's *Alice Doesn't Live Here Anymore*), Cybill Shepherd (the beautiful ex-

model and a frequent star in Peter Bogdanovich's films) and Peter Boyle. *Bang the Drum Slowly* also brought Michael Moriarty into the American front line, and British audiences have the chance to register their feelings after seeing *Report to the Commissioner.*

American actors frequently say how they envy British actors the ease with which they move from films to theatre to television without affecting their career detrimentally. But perhaps that ease of movement is itself deceptive for few British actors achieve the kind of international stardom of Brando, Redford or Caan. Those actors who achieve great things on the stage are not often the ones who create sparks on celluloid.

"I'm quite prepared to believe that actors are right to think directors are notoriously blinkered and unimaginative," says John Schlesinger. "I think we are, quite often. But actors never realise that screen acting is something indefinable. They say. 'Oh, I could play that part, I'm a good actor.' But that just isn't the answer. It's the reason that quite a number have been plucked from nowhere and become stars with very little experience. I can't say what stardom is, except that you recognise it when you see it up there. Neither can I prophesy because stardom is also a question of the sales machine."

The link, then, is charisma: a quality which alters subtly from one star to another, and from one generation to another and yet remains ever present, indefinable, magical. "The quality that the camera likes," was how Dirk Bogarde once described it. And it is a fact that every major star and every embryo star, must have an enduring love affair with the camera lens if he is to survive.

Above: Robert DeNiro in The Godfather Part II. Above left: Michael Moriarty with Yaphet Kotto in Report to the Commissioner. Opposite page: Malcolm McDowell and Florinda Bolkan in Royal Flash

Echoes of the Past

Kenneth Thompson

Opposite page:
Robert
Redford in
The Great
Waldo
Pepper

The demise of the cinema as both an inexpensive and family entertainment; the disappearance of the regular filmgoing habit, allied with the rise of television as cinema substitute; the collapse of the studio system ... such are the most obvious reasons accounting for the gradual but steady change over the past decade or so in the overall climate of film-making. Yet some of the old genres and traditions have not entirely vanished, and there even appears to be a substratum of production which consciously looks to the past.

In its most extreme form, it is a matter of outright remake, a standard enough process in the film industry and one which is a temptation that few of the major studios have been able to resist. Yet it is surprising indeed to be presented in 1975 with a remake of *The Front Page* (1931), one of the first stage-derived, all-dialogue classics of the early talkies. Even less predictable was that MGM would contemplate, leave alone carry out, a remake of their once remarkable venture into authentic locale African adventure, *Trader Horn* (1931). Their similar location piece, *King Solomon's Mines* (1950), allied with the emergence of the new *Trader Horn,* might suggest that MGM are bent on a long-term African cycle whose constituents appear every other

decade. Not that the 1931 version had much in common with the almost unfilmable book from which it took its title (nor, for that matter, did their version of *King Solomon's Mines* bear much resemblance to Rider Haggard), but the delay in presenting the new *Trader Horn* in Britain makes one wonder what on earth they have done with it this time.

Any hopes that *The Ghoul* (1975) would be a remake of the Boris Karloff British-made shudderer of 1933 were dashed when, instead of Karloff's demented Egyptologist with a jewel that he believes will invest him with immortality, it is Peter Cushing as an ex-priest with a human-flesh-eating son who is fed on this extraordinary diet up in the attic by the Hindu housekeeper.

But at least the horror film has received a just enough tribute in Mel Brooks's *Young Frankenstein* (1974), a parody at once affectionate and accurate, accomplished with respect for its original, James Whale's *Frankenstein* (1931). It is tempting to wonder what might have been done with *The Bride of Frankenstein* (1935), a rare instance of a sequel being incomparably better than its predecessor, and moreover a film which probably presents greater possibilities for parody treatment.

One would have thought that the comic-

strip style of the serials of the '30s and '40s would lend itself ideally to such treatment, but in practice, evidently, this seems difficult to sustain. *Flesh Gordon* (1974) took the easier course of updated eroticised parody, whereas *Doc Savage* (1975) pursued the more difficult path of comparatively "straight" approach. Even *Young Frankenstein* was patchy in its effect: the genre is recalcitrant, it seems.

The appeal of dinosaurs rampaging across the screen remains little diminished. The film career of representatives of the giant reptiles may have been intermittent since Willis O'Brien created the prototypes in *The Lost World* (1925) — and these still look impressive despite half a century of progress in special-effects work — but at any rate it is a career of undoubted longevity. *The Land That Time Forgot* (1974) has only a minor stake in dinosaurs among its plethora of imaginative visuals, but sufficient at any rate to maintain the tradition. Meantime it is good to see a long overdue attempt to do something like justice to Edgar Rice Burroughs.

I doubt if we have seen the last of dinosaurs yet. And hopefully we haven't seen the last of the film musical either, even though the halcyon years of the genre have long since gone.

The screen has for some time rested content almost entirely with adaptations of the big stage hits. If it has proved itself a success in the theatre, the chances are it will make a commercially viable film: such would appear to be the prevailing motto, and commercially such reasoning seems to have worked well enough whether the original is saccharine-sweet or hard-rock. In this play-safe, no-originality approach, the cinema is merely reflecting the musical stage which similarly has long been content to seek the groundwork in pre-existing material, raiding sources from George Bernard Shaw to Colette, H G Wells to Charles Dickens.

Change has come, at long last, with Peter Bogdanovich's *At Long Last Love*, a musical designed specifically and written directly for the screen: as tit for tat, a stage version in due course might not be inappropriate. The "nostalgia" of the film has been much commented on, but to my mind any such traits are more illusory than real.

True, its story material, plot devices and character deployment stem from old formulae, the affinity being more specifically with the Astaire-Rogers films: indeed, with little alteration, the plot substance could have formed a characteristic enough subject for these two stars with the participation of Edward Everett Horton, Erik

Rhodes and Co. But in other respects it defies rather than recollects the old conventions. The Cole Porter songs are in the heart of the film, but the exceptionally large line-up is a contemporary fancy, a novelty even, owing little or nothing to '30s musicals.

Any film-maker would today be hard put to find stars experienced in film musical traditions, simply because such traditions have all but disappeared since the golden years of the MGM musicals came to an end; but in opting for a cast with such indifferent singing voices, Bogdanovich follows a modern theatrical trend in evidence since the days when theatregoers were startled to find such "straight" players as Herbert Lom and Valerie Hobson cast in a Drury Lane musical.

It might be argued that, despite his many recordings, Fred Astaire's singing voice was

unremarkable (Ginger's even less), but in compensation was the fact that Fred was a stylist with an individual, inimitable way of putting over a song. In any event, it was the dance sequences which were the mainstay of the Astaire-Rogers films, whereas the cast of *At Long Last Love* are hardly able to do more than get through their dance routines ("Some very heavy hoofing" as one critic put it).

The story has a 1935 setting, belied by the modern musical arrangements and orchestrations. And the avoidance of a conventional "happy ending" in favour of an open-ended fade-out is, again, a contemporary conceit quite opposed to old-time practice which would have demanded either a joy-for-all or a bitter-sweet (Jeanette MacDonald-Nelson Eddy style) ending.

The film's self-conscious but certainly effective experiments in colour and design —

Above: Jack Nicholson in Chinatown. Opposite page: Cybill Shepherd and Burt Reynolds in At Long Last Love

black and white in a colour environment — is another factor which makes it much a film of the '70s. Still, ending excepted, the story is quite like old times. Even more like old times, of course, was the direct recapitulation of the past in MGM's large-scale compilation *That's Entertainment* (1974), though the paste-and-scissors approach would seem to have limited possibilities. If skilfully done, compilations of Universal's horror films or Warner Bros.' *films noirs* of the '40s could make entertaining viewing, and perhaps dedicated fans would welcome *The Best of the Durango Kid*, but it's difficult to foresee any appreciable development along these lines. Or will the example of *Airport, The Godfather* and *The French Connection* be followed so that we get *That's Entertainment, Part II?*

Right, top: Gene Wilder and Peter Boyle as the Creature in Young Frankenstein. Bottom: Colin Clive and John Boles in the James Whale Frankenstein (1931)

With its 1937 setting, *Chinatown* (1974) has been much acclaimed as a contemporary film of vintage quality. The private-eye type of thriller, which flourished particularly in the '40s, has become a comparatively rare bird in latter-day cinema, if continuing to be familiar in the world of television films. With the success of *Chinatown,* plus the remake of *Farewell My Lovely* (yet to be seen at the time of writing), the prospect of a return to favour does not seem particularly remote.

Tony Richardson's *Dead Cert* (1974) had the effect of reviving a long-neglected genre. In the mid-'20s, when the British film industry was in a particularly moribund state, "dramas of the turf" abounded. Evidently there was a public for them, and in the field of popular literature the racing stories of Nat Gould were as ubiquitous as the thrillers of Edgar Wallace (himself no mean writer of horseracing fiction). The spate of horseracing films ended with the advent of the talkies, thereafter dwindling to only occasional ventures into turf territory. The only survivor was the film which virtually climaxed the horseracing binge, Edgar Wallace's *The Calendar* (1931), which proved its staying power by being honoured with a remake in 1948 by Gainsborough, though the new version did not noticeably revive interest in the genre. Dick Francis's novels may be a world away from the racing stories of Gould or Wallace, but in its crime and turf material *Dead Cert* clearly belongs to an old and almost defunct tradition in film-making.

Sidney Lumet's *Murder on the Orient Express* (1974), which so quickly proved itself a box-office bonanza, is founded on basic material as old as that of *Dead Cert.* Like Bogdanovich's musical and *Chinatown,* its story is set in the '30s, contemporaneously with the Agatha Christie book on which it was based. Its ancestry as a mystery-thriller with a railway train setting is long and honourable: *The Lady Vanishes* (1938) is its most obvious but far from only precursor. Being an Agatha Christie subject, the thriller element inclines towards the "whodunnit" style. In a review of the film, Penelope Houston suggested that the screen has never been much good at classic detection "with its detached deductive processes and apparatus of alibis and time-tables." A valid argument, though if the cinema is not much good at it, want of trying is plainly not the reason.

For at least two decades, the screen was congested with detectives, demonstrating their deductive processes, usually contriving at the finish to gather their suspects together in order to expose the guilty party. Sleuths of every ilk, from the orchid-hothouse brainstorms of Nero Wolfe to the sophisticated elegance of Nick Charles, plus the more prosaic investigations of sundry caricatured Scotland Yard Inspectors and Superintendents, went through the motions. The silent film had plenty of thrillers, but the unequivocal "whodunnit" style did not develop in strength until the advent of the talkies, simply because the type of "apparatus" to which Ms Houston refers demanded dialogue to be more than marginally effective; and even with the benefit of sound the cinema was unable to cope with the "time-table" complexities of, say, Freeman Wills Croft.

Nevertheless, the "whodunnit" was staple diet for the filmgoer of the '30s and '40s. Similarly, the train-set thriller did not develop appreciably until much the same time (for no readily apparent reason — it just happened that way), but it stemmed from the largely American genre that for convenience I will term the railroad drama.

Ever since Lumière's 1896 train arrived in its station, the cinema has been constantly fascinated by the paraphernalia of railways and the motion of locomotives. In the early years, when the one or two reel film held full sway, the Kalem company, for instance, had its own track and stock handy for its numerous requirements in this direction. The best survivor is probably *The Grit of the Girl Telegrapher* (1913), starring Anna Q Nilsson, if only because it has long been available for the delectation of home-movie collectors.

The genre continued to flourish in the early silent serials during the heyday of Pearl White, Ruth Roland and, especially, Helen Holmes, who emerged as the queen of the railroad film. When feature-length productions took control, it became mainly the prerogative of the smaller companies: of the major studios, only Universal displayed any consistent interest. The majority of these films were centred on strictly railway personnel — engine drivers, firemen, signalmen or station staff. The "boss" (president, manager or, at least, superintendent) was an essential character, either directly as a principal protagonist, or indirectly because the boss's son/daughter is hero/heroine of the drama (the superintendent's daughter was a standard role for Helen Holmes, though on one occasion at least she was promoted to the status of a lady superintendent!).

By 1927, the craze was for runaway coaches, customarily entailing the last-minute rescue of the heroine: for example, *Wolf's Clothing* and *The Black Diamond Express* (both 1927, with Monte Blue) and a Marie Prevost film *The Girl in the Pullman* (1927). This old-style railroad drama survived the transitional period from silent films to talkies, but in addition to American contributions such as *The Crash* (1928) and *The Greyhound Limited* (1929), British studios now got into the act, responding with *The Wrecker* (1929), *The Flying Scotsman* (1931) and two versions of *The Ghost Train* (1927 and 1931).

Then the railway-set thriller began to get into its stride. In *The Night Express* (1932), two thieves plan to steal a necklace when mixing with guests at a masquerade ball, but encounter a fellow ex-con with much the same objective in mind. The latter is murdered aboard a train, and a number of passengers come under suspicion. *By Whose Hand* (1932) was set on an express Pullman

train and starred Ben Lyon as a reporter out to get a story about an escaped convict believed to be among the passengers, who include the reporter's girl, a wealthy jeweller, another ex-convict, a squealer, a girl drug-addict and the convict's wife who is in disguise and is travelling with a coffin in which her husband is hidden! The jeweller is murdered and the drug-addict, who has stolen a bracelet from him, becomes prime suspect. Then the squealer is murdered, so too are the train's driver and fireman with the result that the train goes out of control (thus introducing a touch of the older-style railroad drama).

British studios responded to this new development with the well-known *Rome Express* (1932), a railway thriller which foreshadowed *Murder on the Orient Express,* for the Paris-Rome express is little different for screen purposes from the Paris-Istanbul express, and the obligatory assortment of passengers even includes a detective who, if not in Poirot's class, is nevertheless the French investigator of the affair.

The Silk Express (1933) had Guy Kibbee as the detective in a murder-on-the-train story, the crime taking place in a freight car and involving a paralysed witness who knows the identity of the killer. The sleuth prevents an attack on the paralytic in a tunnel and identifies the murderer before the train arrives in New York. *Orient Express* (1934), like the 1974 film, is set on the famous train, although the journey is in the opposite direction: the plot involves a dancer, a Balkan communist, a newspaper reporter and an international thief.

A lively mixture of the old and new styles was *Murder on the Runaway Train* (1934), starring Charles Ruggles and Una Merkel, in which a telephone operator finds she is the daughter of a railroad millionaire. She is kidnapped and taken aboard a private railroad car, but the kidnapper is murdered on the train and the private car is cut loose by the millionaire's mad brother. The girl is rescued by a criminologist in an exciting final reel, culminating in the last-minute escape from the runaway rolling-stock. The traditional participation of millionaires and railway officials still persisted, and remnants even survive in *Murder on the Orient Express* since the characters include both a millionaire and a railway executive.

Silver Streak (1935) centred on a young railroad engineer who has designed a high-speed streamline train, finally having the chance to test it on a non-stop run to transport medical equipment to save the life of the railroad president's son. The train, of course, smashes all speed records. This temporary return to the older style was also in evidence at much the same time in Britain, in *Cock o' the North* (1935) and, more notably, *The Last Journey* (1936), in which an engine driver facing retirement becomes demented and plans to wreck his train on his last run. Otherwise the railroad drama of the silent days was almost entirely being displaced. *Streamline Express* (1936) hinged on the theft of a diamond pendant and the customary assortment of train passengers, while *Florida Special* (1936) concerned a reporter who discovers that a gang of thieves is out to steal a fortune in jewels being carried by a millionaire (again!) aboard the train.

After *Seven Sinners* (1936), one of the better-known examples of the railway thriller of the time, in which Edmund Lowe played an American detective who, investigating a case of jewel robbery and murder, becomes involved in the mystery of train wrecks, there entered Alfred Hitchcock and *The Lady Vanishes* (1938). "Hitch" had long shown a predilection for subjects containing appreciable railway episodes *(Number Seventeen, The Thirty-Nine Steps, The Secret Agent),* and was to continue to do so more than once in his later Hollywood career. With *The Lady Vanishes,* he made the best-known, classic example of the railway-thriller genre.

It seemed to have a temporarily inhibiting effect, or perhaps it was merely that the possibilities of crime and suspected passengers on a train had already been appreciably exhausted. Certainly the changes rung in the early '40s were unremarkable. *Midnight Limited* (1940) had John King as a railroad detective and Marjorie Reynolds as the heroine in a tale of robbery and murder

aboard a high-speed train, and *Broadway Limited* (1941) found Victor McLaglen in a lighter variation as an engine driver in a comedy about a baby thought to have been kidnapped aboard the train.

With spies and Nazis ubiquitous in the war years, *Spy Train* (1943) was a predictable variation, the thriller element here being provided by a time bomb on the train. After *Night Train to Memphis* (1946), concerning a nefarious railroad president out to do a tricky land deal, the train-thriller concept was given a rest, replaced by a marked revival of interest in the amalgamation of the railroad film and the Western, a combination frequently in evidence since John Ford's *The Iron Horse* (1924).

A cycle of stories about pioneering and railroad construction followed: *Canadian Pacific* (1950), *Transcontinent Express* (1950), *Denver and Rio Grande* (1952), *Kansas Pacific* (1953) and several others. British studios made several films in which railways played a vital yet incidental part, among them *Brief Encounter* (1945), *Waterloo Road* (1945) and *Temptation Harbour* (1947), but interest in the railway thriller had at this time distinctly waned.

What next emerged were some rehashes: Britain did *Sleeping Car to Trieste* (1948), a remake of *Rome Express* and Hollywood, with much the same notion, offered *Peking Express* (1951), a remake of *Shanghai Express* (1932), Josef von Sternberg's distinctive and distinguished production which, all these years later, remains one of the most outstanding of train-centred films.

Shanghai Express had few affiliations with either the disappearing railroad drama or the emerging railway thriller: its blend of romance, adventure and high drama with its train setting and exotic locale (very convincing though completely phoney) had little influence. But after *Peking Express* came two films which substituted India for China and pursued adventure in preference to mystery or "whodunnit" plots for their thrills. *Last Train to Bombay* (1952) concerned a young American diplomat suspected of murder but who is trying to prevent the assassination of an Indian potentate whose train is due to be blown up. In *North West Frontier* (1959), Kenneth More as a British officer is unable to prevent the assassination of another potentate but rescues the latter's son and heads an escape by train. Fluctuating between corny melodrama and genuine suspense, *North West Frontier* had its lighter moments, stemming from the antique locomotive and its cheerfully dedicated driver (engaging played by I S Johar) — under-

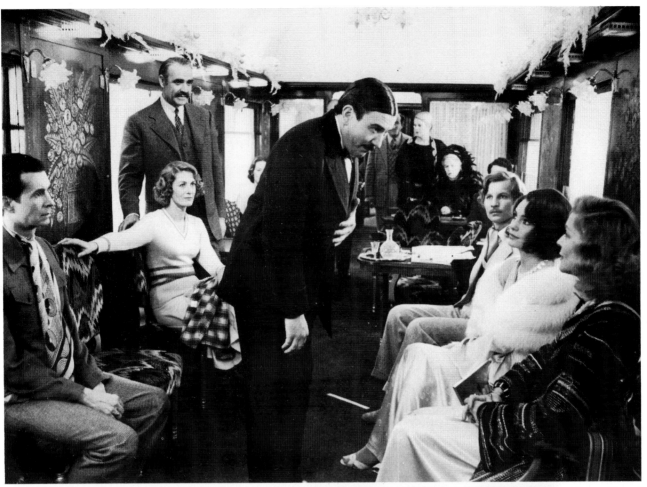

Above: Hercule Poirot questions the suspects in Murder on the Orient Express. Left to right — Anthony Perkins, Vanessa Redgrave, Sean Connery, Albert Finney, Rachel Roberts, Wendy Hiller, Michael York, Jacqueline Bisset and Ingrid Bergman. Left: the Orient Express steams through the countryside

standably, since it seems impossible to use the theme of an ancient locomotive pressed into service without cheerfulness breaking in.

Both *The Titfield Thunderbolt* (1953) and the vintage Will Hay *Oh Mr Porter* (1937) had successfully featured the idea in outright comedy style, and there was an even earlier example in *The Night Flyer* (1928) which concerned an old engine, brought back into service on a mail train, which manages to arrive at its destination *ahead* of time.

The next step was to utilise the adventure style in a war context, *The Train* (1964) and *Von Ryan's Express* (1965). But then it was back to convention and the good old Orient Express again in *Istanbul Express* (1968): direction of travel was this time Paris to Istanbul, but the journey was cut by sixteen minutes for British distribution. Tradition was followed by including a railway official in the principal characters (a security officer in this case), but the story was essentially a secret agent plus missing papers saga which really had less in common with *Murder on the Orient Express* than *Train to Tombstone* (1956), in which the train is carrying a valuable cargo and a robbery attempt is expected. The usual assortment of passengers include a Federal Marshal, an outlaw wanted for murder, a corset sales-man, a doctor, a priest, a dance-hall proprietress, one of her girls, and a young cripple who finds herself attracted to the suspected outlaw and is unconvinced that he is a dangerous killer. It turns out that the Marshal is a fraud, in league with the outlaws who have attacked the train disguised as Indians; the supposed outlaw is in fact an Army officer who, undercover style, has posed as a bad lot in order to expose the gang. Despite its Western setting, this was fundamentally a return to the railway thriller of the '30s.

Rivalling, even exceeding, railways in fascination for the film-maker are aircraft. Both *Airport* (1969) – plus, of course, its successor *Airport 1975* – and *The Great Waldo Pepper* (1975) have in their different ways roots in mainstream developments of the air film. Stunts with aircraft provided a thrilling condiment for many a silent serial from *The Perils of Pauline* (1914) onwards, and by the mid '20s the feature-film format centred on movies featuring air stunt specialist Al Wilson. Such exciting diversions (for the time) as fights on the wings of planes, exploits with rope ladders, and such climactic scenes as changing an aeroplane wheel in mid-air were the highspots of simple adventure or melodramatic stories. They reached their apex in 1927 and 1928

when Wilson had come under the aegis of Universal, who issued a steady stream of them. The air film soon developed into several well defined, if sometimes inter-related types, which might be summed up as (1) civil or commercial aviation, (2) military aviation, (3) disaster and rescue, (4) research and testing, (5) stunting and racing. Of these, the first has always enjoyed numerical supremacy. It began to develop in earnest in the mid '20s when the especially favourite theme was the airmail service, then in its infancy and accordingly an up-to-date subject. Treatment has, with appreciable consistency, tended to take the form of melodrama, from the silent days right up to *Skyjacked* (1972) and *Airport 1975*.

In *The Airmail* (1925), starring Warner Baxter and Douglas Fairbanks Jnr, a pilot in league with a gang of thieves gets a job in the airmail service with larceny in view until romance and other considerations lead him to turn over a new leaf: he turns on his ex-associates after they attack his plane. Al Wilson made his contribution in *The Flying Mail* (1926), while Charles Hutchison did similar stunts in *Pirates of the Sky* (1927) as a pilot engaged to round up mail service thieves. Very similar was *Flying High* (1927), in which William Fairbanks portrayed an airman, in love with the boss's daughter, who apprehends airmail bandits – headed, it turns out, by the company's transport manager. Company executives and the boss's offspring were, incidentally, almost as ubiquitous in the air film as in the railroad drama, and the company chief who proves to be the villain was a variation used

more than once. *The Air Legion* (1929) found Antonio Moreno and Ben Lyon in a mail service story which ended with one pilot rescuing a crashed colleague and carrying medical supplies to an isolated area in the teeth of a tornado.

By the early '30s, the formerly simple stories were giving way to more ornate concoctions. *Air Mail* (1932), with Pat O'Brien and Ralph Bellamy, concerned a stunt flyer who becomes an airmail pilot. His superintendent, while flying a mission, crashes in the mountains, is spotted from the air but cannot be reached, and is accordingly theatened by death from exposure. But it's Pat O'Brien to the rescue.

Much more ambitious was *Night Flight* (1933), a story of the early days of night mail flying, with a splendid MGM cast headed by Lionel Barrymore, Clark Gable, Robert Montgomery, Helen Hayes and Myrna Loy. One flyer battles his way home, another loses his way in a storm and is forced to jump to his death, another delivers a serum to save a child's life. Besides the flying through fogs, storms and blizzards, over mountains and sea, and the parachute descents which were considered quite a thrill and were almost obligatory in air films of this period, there was also the type of nerve-wracking tension on the ground at the airline's headquarters, to become a familiar dramatic ingredient over the years. Gable, incidentally, was described as "never being seen outside of his aeroplane and has only a few words to shout above the din of his engine."

Night Flight virtually brought this early cycle to an end, for as airmail became a commonplace in reality, its fascination as a subject for film makers decreased — though Columbia made a later if major contribution in *Only Angels Have Wings* (1939), featuring Cary Grant and Jean Arthur in a story of a struggling airmail service in South America.

By the mid '30s, the shift of emphasis was from airmail to passenger flights, bringing with it an increase in the disaster/rescue motif, which had already been an important factor in *Night Flight* and on occasion had formed almost a separate genre in *The Lost Zeppelin* (1930) and Frank Capra's *Dirigible* (1931), both about airship catastrophes in icy conditions. Contrast between incident in the air and control on the ground became prominent, and has remained so ever since. In *Without Orders* (1936), Sally Eilers is a stewardess left in charge of a plane when the pilot loses his nerve in a storm and jumps to his death: she safely lands the plane by radio instruction from Robert Armstrong. Similar in theme was *Flying Hostess* (1936) which had Judith Barrett as the stewardess who distinguishes herself by bringing the plane safely down after the pilot has been knocked out.

Pursuing a different course and providing the sort of romantic complication which later became part of the stock-in-trade of many air films, more notably the larger-scale or bumper-bundle productions (including *Airport*), was *The Man Who Found Himself* (1936). John Beal played a doctor who is a keen flyer until his plane crashes and his woman passenger is killed. He then abandons his career and becomes an airport mechanic. An ambulance-plane nurse (Joan Fontaine) becomes attracted to him but is unable to induce him to return to the medical profession. However, when she is involved in a train crash, he is called upon to fly the ambulance-plane and finally performs an emergency operation.

An airport theme was central to *Flight at Midnight* (1939), starring Phil Reagan, Jean Parker and Robert Armstrong. The airport is, somewhat curiously, surrounded by high-tension wires, which for obvious reasons of safety are supposed to be converted into underground cables — but the airport is short of funds. At the climax, a test pilot deliberately crashes his plane into the wires so as to save the lives of passengers aboard an airliner which has developed engine trouble.

With the outbreak of World War II, the civil aviation film understandably took a dive, and the cycle virtually ended with *Flight Angels* (1940), with Virginia Bruce playing an air hostess in a cast which also included Dennis Morgan, Wayne Morris, Ralph Bellamy and Jane Wyman. But a new spate erupted in 1957 with *Zero Hour* and continued for several years. In *Zero Hour*, Dana Andrews played a wartime pilot who was responsible for the death of his crew and who in peacetime has to take control of an airliner when its pilot succumbs to food poisoning; he is guided down by Sterling Hayden as the control-tower officer. In *Crash Landing* (1958), Gary Merrill was the airliner captain forced to crash-land in the sea, while Dana Andrews returned to the flight deck controls in *The Crowded Sky* (1960) as the airliner pilot on collision course with a Navy jet plane.

Meantime, Britain had contributed *Jet Storm* (1959), in which a motley assortment of passengers are menaced by Richard Attenborough as a maniac with a hidden bomb, and *Cone of Silence* (1960) with Bernard Lee as a pilot accused of error which resulted in a crash. *Jet Over the Atlantic* (1959, British release 1961) was

America's counterpart to *Jet Storm,* with a transatlantic flight menaced by a psychopath who has smuggled a bomb aboard, and further embellishment of the bomb theme formed part of the story make-up of the recent *Skyjacked.* Ralph Nelson's *Fate is the Hunter* (1964), with a crash investigation story, was of much the same school as *Cone of Silence,* with Rod Taylor as the pilot, Suzanne Pleshette as the stewardess survivor finally ably to clear his name, and Glenn Ford as an airline director. The way was clear for the two highly popular *Airport* films, firmly rooted in the tradition of the civil aviation genre.

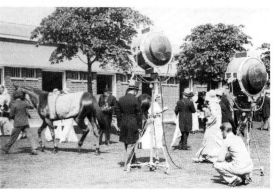

The Great Waldo Pepper derives principally from the branch of the air film which I have termed stunting and racing, though it owes something, too, to the films about World War I combat. These latter were comparatively few in number but tended to be on a large scale since they called for big production resources. The outstanding earlier examples are William Wellman's *Wings* (1927), which won renewed critical acclaim when revived in London not long ago, the two versions of *The Dawn Patrol* (1930, with Richard Barthelmess; 1939, with Errol Flynn), and the now almost legendary *Hell's Angels* (1930), which excited me to the core as a boy and which I was fortunate enough to see several times before the war in the original tinted print — unhappily, word has it that the complete version no longer exists. The genre has had relatively recent additions in *The Blue Max* (1966) and *The Red Baron* (1971), again both large-scale productions. *Wings* and its immediate successors had some indirect influence on other main branches of the air film in that the figure of a wartime air ace turned peacetime flyer became a standard character in the '30s, in most instances becoming either a barnstorming pilot in an air circus or a test pilot, thereby giving rise to two conspicuous branches of the air film, those concerning stunting and racing, and those about research and testing.

The latter group, hinging on test piloting and the development of new gadgets and techniques, began in the mid '30s. *Wings in the Dark* (1935) had Myrna Loy as a stunt flyer and Cary Grant as an aviator who has invented instruments to facilitate blind flying but loses his sight. The denouement comes when the girl gets into difficulties in a non-stop flight from Moscow to the United States, and the blind flyer takes off to help her, proving the efficacy of his invention.

One of the James Cagney-Pat O'Brien movies, *Ceiling Zero* (1936) involved an airline superintendent who gives a job to his wild pilot pal of Great War days. Having caused a disaster, the pilot makes good by taking up a plane in a storm to test a new de-icing invention. Another example was *Devil's Squadron* (1936), with Richard Dix as a test pilot concerned with a new aircraft, intended for Government service, testing of which has resulted in a succession of fatal accidents. MGM's big production *Test Pilot* (1938), with Clark Gable, Myrna Loy and Spencer Tracy, was the peak of the '30s cycle, but it seemed to have a stultifying effect on its successors which tended to pursue a more melodramatic course, usually involving spies or crooks after the plans of the new device or plane.

With the outbreak of World War II, the emphasis shifted to the training of recruits at such establishments as the Pensacola Naval Air Training Station. The blueprint for this development had already appeared: *Wings of the Navy* (1938). George Brent played an instructor who has invented a new device but, injured in a crash, has to leave the testing to his younger brother (John Payne). *20,000 Men a Year* (1939) and several others followed. Nevertheless, the mainstream of test pilot films continued, with or without the participation of spies (*Power Dive,* 1941; *Emergency Landing,* 1941), and sometimes the two types were combined — for instance in *Flying Cadets* (1941), starring Edmund Lowe as an air ace and soldier of fortune, in which a flying-school cadet takes up a plane with a new-type engine known to be faulty, or *Dive Bomber* (1941), a big entry from Warner Bros. with a cast to match (Errol Flynn, Fred MacMurray, Ralph Bellamy,

Alexis Smith, Robert Armstrong), set at San Diego Navy Air Base and concerning experiments to solve the problem of blackouts by pilots in high-altitude flying.

Dive Bomber had a close relation in another Warner Bros. film, *Chain Lightning* (1950), starring Humphrey Bogart, Eleanor Parker and Raymond Massey, and by this time it was a question of supersonic flight. Bogart plays a wartime bomber pilot who on demobilisation has a struggle to become a test pilot for a new jet. Working with him is an aircraft designer who was with him on his last mission over Germany and is now trying to increase safety in high-altitude flight.

Over the next few years there was a spate of similar films, from "B" pictures such as *Jet Job* (1952) to major productions. These included the well-known *The Sound Barrier* (1952) and its virtual successor *The Net* (1953); *On the Threshold of Space* (1956), about medical scientists' research into problems posed by high altitude flight and a new ejector seat; *Bale Out at 43,000* (1957), another variation on a new high-altitude ejector seat; *Brink of Hell* (1956), concerning experimental research and test piloting, centred on a suspected wing defect; and *Destination 60,000* (1957), about test piloting for an aircraft construction company building a new jet plane which uses a revolutionary fuel.

The stunt flyer was as familiar a figure as the test pilot, and to this branch of the air film *The Great Waldo Pepper* is particularly indebted. Two of the earliest films in the cycle were *The Air Circus* (1928) in which the central characters were two pals who become flyers, plus a daring girl aviator, and *Air Eagles* (1931) involving two wartime pilots who find employment as stunters in an air circus. *The Lost Squadron* (1931) was a major film from Radio with a cast to match (Richard Dix, Robert Armstrong, Joel McCrea, Erich von Stroheim, Mary Astor) and was one of the very few specifically about stunt flying for Hollywood films — a major story ingredient in *The Great Waldo Pepper*.

Two years later, Radio made another film which finds an echo or two in *Waldo: The Flying Circus* (1933), which featured Ralph Bellamy and Bruce Cabot as members of a group of exhibition flyers in an air circus, performing daring exploits and stunt flying, while the wife (Arline Judge) of one of them does a spectacular parachute jump. Moreover, two of the pilots arrange a new collision stunt in which both will leave their planes only seconds before the crash.

Meantime, Paramount had contributed *Sky Bride* (1932), another about a flying circus,

with Richard Arlen as a daredevil-type pilot who crashes into the plane piloted by his friend who is killed. Haunted by the tragedy brought about by his recklessness, he vows never to fly again and becomes a mechanic in an aircraft factory — until he finds that a plane has taken off with a small child who, unnoticed, has climbed on to the aircraft.

Other members of the cycle included a Mascot serial, *The Shadow of the Eagle* (1931), in which John Wayne played a stunt flyer (an ex-war pilot, of course) who now runs an air circus, and *Parachute Jumper* (1932) in which Douglas Fairbanks and Bette Davis were involved in a tale of an ex-Marine who finds employment by giving exhibition jumps. Another Radio film, *Men Against the Sky* (1940), with Richard Dix and Edmund Lowe, is interesting in combining this trend with the test piloting school as well as with the less frequently encountered air race theme, occasionally used as an alternative to stunting. The story concerns a stunter who takes to drink and is thus unable to find employment. He gets a job on the staff of an aircraft construction company whose future depends on its winning a competition for a fast pursuit plane. A test reveals that there is a defect: the wings come off during a steep dive. But a subsequent test is successful until the landing gear jams, whereupon the ex-pilot takes up a plane in an effort to correct the fault but loses his life in the process.

Another film which blended two standard themes was *The Flight Command* (1940), with Robert Taylor as a pilot fresh from Pensacola who joins the Hell Cats, yet the story turns substantially into a research and testing variant after an officer is killed trying out, contrary to orders, an invention designed to facilitate safe landings in fog: Taylor eventually proves the device and saves the life of Squadron Commander Walter Pidgeon.

The flying-circus story went almost totally out of fashion until *The Tarnished Angels* (1957), an adaptation of William Faulkner's novel Pylon, about an ace pilot of World War I who becomes a stunt flyer in fairgrounds during the Depression years. A direct return, in other words, to the old tradition, though an isolated instance until *The Great Waldo Pepper*.

So, there is plenty of precedent for *Airport*; Waldo's aerobatics and pseudo-dogfight is in the grand manner of old; and despite the sophistication of today's cinema, *Murder on the Orient Express* conforms to the procedure which no railway film has been able to resist for over fifty years — it is full of cuts to the train in motion. *Plus ca change* . . .

Laughter in the Dark

David Castell

Comedy is the informer. Nothing else in the field of entertainment tells us so much about the age that bore it; nothing else reflects so accurately the modes and mores of the day.

Movie buffs will sit up all night and argue which was the golden age of screen comedy — the silent years or the sophisticated era of the late '30s and '40s. But there is agreement on one thing: the steady decline in post-war years.

For my money, the American film comedy didn't hit rock bottom until the late '50s or early '60s. The last decade has been a desert, the occasional oasis inevitably turning out to be a mirage.

The last cycle of any moment was the Universal sex comedy *(Pillow Talk, Lover Come Back, That Touch of Mink* etcetera) in which euphemism ruled triumphant, and Doris Day found more excuses for *not* going to bed with Rock Hudson than ever she could have made apologies for capitulating.

There was an arch coyness endemic to the early '60s. Comedy was assumed by definition to be a family affair. It was as unthinkable that anything really *risqué* should shatter the mirrored calm of these placid bedroom fantasies as it was to imagine Doris Day going to bed in curlers or waking up in the morning without fresh lipstick.

The one attempt to broaden the appeal of the series and make the films more adult, in *A Very Special Favour,* resulted in an X rating. Whether this was on account of Rock Hudson's pose as a homosexual (in order to insinuate himself with seeming harmlessness into Leslie Caron's boudoir) or whether it was the tastelessness of the deceit in the seduction, this is still open to question. A mere decade on, the controversy seems feeble and puerile. Comedy is no longer the starchily laundered affair it was.

The America of the '60s was hurtling lemming-like towards social, sexual and moral precipices. Landmarks along that route are pointed out by such iconoclastic, but isolated, films as *Bob & Carol & Ted & Alice* (psychological), *M*A*S*H* (sociological) and the later *Shampoo* (sexual/political).

It was no longer tenable for a sexually liberated audience to accept the bashful fantasies of Hudson, Day, Cary Grant, Tony Randall, Gig Young and other members of the Universal repertory company. The characters they played were too impossibly well bred, the conduct too flawlessly becoming.

An early warning of the wind of change came from the undervalued team of Norman Lear and Bud Yorkin. In *Divorce American Style* they had taken the formula sex comedy characters and breathed a little fire

Opposite page, top: Teri Garr, Gene Wilder, Madeline Kahn in Young Frankenstein. Bottom: Diane Keaton and Woody Allen in Play It Again, Sam

into their bellies. But with the aptly titled *Start the Revolution Without Me* they broke down and revalued a lot of the basic concepts on which movie comedy was built. This freer, zanier style gave rein to an actor who was quickly to become one of the seminal figures in the new comedy.

Gene Wilder had made a notable contribution to *Bonnie and Clyde*, as the nervous Texas undertaker, Eugene Grizzard, but it was with *Start the Revolution Without Me* that he found his real forte. Playing twins, one good and one evil (the very schizophrenia of the part helped shape his own personal comedy of anxiety), he gave us here our first chance to acquire a taste for the hysteria, the paranoia, the towering rages that are equal ingredients of his unfettered style.

The film also proved, importantly, that it was possible to break social taboos (some jokes revolving around a blind man) without alienating the audience. Also that this audience would not lose its capacity for pathos amid the lunatic gallivanting. The most touching scene in the film involves Hugh Griffith's cruelly put-upon Louis who mingles with his exquisitely gowned guests while himself wearing a chicken costume. "They told me it was fancy dress," he mutters apologetically in a broad Welsh accent, as the courtiers bow and scrape, pretending not to notice his *faux pas*.

But the film itself passed without too much comment (though it subsequently went underground and still enjoys a wide cult success with young audiences today) and Yorkin, having planted the seed, meandered off into the softer and safer territory of the glossy caper comedy with *The Thief Who Came to Dinner*.

Around the same time, a British distributor very cautiously tested *Take the Money and Run*, the first film as overall *auteur* by Woody Allen, whom audiences had received with containable fervour in *What's New, Pussycat?* and the even more disorienting *Casino Royale*. A former gag writer, Allen had enjoyed a big success in American cabaret where his lugubrious comedy won him a firm following. He talked nervously about his intense desire to return to the womb —anybody's — about his father, who used to work in a factory but was replaced by a small gadget. His mother, he said, bought one. "Time" described this woeful comedian as, "a flat-headed, red-haired lemur with closely bitten fingernails and a sports jacket." For the cinema, Allen made himself no more charismatic. His pose as the neurotic, bespectacled weakling made for a strange kind of hero, but *angst* was something with which analysis-ridden audiences could readily identify.

The third significant breakthrough was that of Mel Brooks with his monument to bad taste, *The Producers*. That film found more hostility than applause on its first release. Indeed, it remains the least even of Brooks' films. But Peter Sellers disagreed and lent his testimonial to the advertising campaign: "Last night I saw the ultimate film... brilliantly written and directed by Mel Brooks, it is the essence of all great comedy combined in a single motion picture. Without any doubt, Mel Brooks displays true genius in weaving together tragi-comedy, comedy-tragedy, pity, fear, hysteria, schizophrenia and a largess of lunacy with sheer magic. The casting is perfect. Those of us who have seen this film and understood it have experienced a phenomenon which occurs only once in a life span".

These were the prophets without honour. Initially they were prophets without profit as well, but hindsight finally encouraged us to line their pockets.

Comedy had crossed over from being part of the problem to being part of the solution. It had been mobilised and sent into battle. There was fire, sass and vinegar as film-makers set out to lead audiences rather than follow them.

The sick joke had already been guiltily accepted as cathartic and it was now taken to fresh extremes. Brooks in particular attacked taboos with rare fervour. Being Jewish himself, he knows the description of Jewish humour as, "laughter on the brink of the grave." He himself tap-danced through a minefield with *The Producers*, the seeming folly of which exercise won him some stunned admiration.

This was not so much black comedy as laughter in the dark. The Jew who dared to make a musical comedy joke about Nazism (the film's original title was "Springtime For Hitler," and that song remains one of the highspots) and take some potent sideswipes at other forbidden topics was not short on nerve or *chutzpah*. "I look at my films," Brooks reflects, "and I think, 'Am I that vulgar? Am I that Jewish?' And the answer is: yes, I am. You can only be your true self in a film. I give you myself, you give me two quid. That's the deal."

The story of *The Producers* is that of a timid accountant, Leo Bloom (Gene Wilder) who falls into company with an unethical Broadway producer, Max Bialystock (Zero Mostel). Bloom points out that by dramatically overfinancing a surefire flop, a producer could become extremely rich. "I

meant no scheme. I merely posed a little academic accounting theory," he says defensively, but Bialystock has the bit between his teeth and quickly seduces Bloom away from his grey, meaningless life.

"I want — I want — I want everything I've ever seen in the movies!" Leo cries deliriously, as floodlit fountains jet their celebration of his liberation. For their flop they choose the musical "Springtime for Hitler" and hire a hopeless, homosexual director. Bialystock raises a fortune by seducing elderly ladies ("one last fling on the way to the cemetery") but of course the show is a runaway success. After Bialystock has tried literally to undermine it, by blowing up the theatre, he and Bloom are sent to jail, only to spring a similar scheme with a prison revue.

"*The Producers* didn't take off too well because it was very insular," says Brooks. "You had to know a certain amount about Broadway, a certain amount about homosexuality. I think those things mitigated against it." Although the film

Left: Zero Mostel and Gene Wilder in The Producers. Below: Madeline Kahn in Blazing Saddles

looks forward in its grit and iconoclasm, it also abounds in references to the past. The actual "Springtime For Hitler" number is a little gem of staging — goose-stepping showgirls grouping in swastika formation like the dancers in a Busby Berkeley musical. In his subsequent films, Brooks was more fully to indulge his sense of parody; his work was to become more firmly and affectionately anchored in the past.

Woody Allen shares Brooks' basic nostalgia and, although his humour is not as caustic, there is a wealth of references in *Take the Money and Run, Bananas* and *Play It Again, Sam* — the film he let Herbert Ross make of his own stage play, and in which he starred as a timid film critic with a Humphrey Bogart fixation. In this more than any other film, Allen finds his true persona — the sexual incompetent, riddled with anxieties and totally unable to cope with the consumer society. ("Who bothers to cook frozen dinners?" he asks a neighbour. "I suck them frozen.") Although the script is peppered with agile wisecracks, the tone of Allen's character is that of plaintive despair. "I'm twenty-nine. The height of my sexual potency was ten years ago!" he wails. But with excitement comes confusion. "I love you Miss Whoever-You-Are, I want to have your baby," he chants to the blonde he has been secretly ogling. Her answer is

crisp and inevitable: "Get lost, creep!".

His most ambitious film was probably *Sleeper,* which was set 200 years into the future, a time in which Allen sees himself as the only man with a normal sex drive in a dictatorship of sexless uniformity. The character is a modern Rip Van Winkle, a health food fanatic who had himself put on ice in 1973, only to awaken to an even worse world.

His neuroses adjust immediately to the time-lag. His primary concern is the staggering amount of arrears owing in National Insurance contributions. His secondary concern is to avoid the brainwashing that will quench his sex drive ("My brain!" he cries in horror. "It's my second favourite organ.") Stress and anxiety fears could not meet a nightmare more vivid that a 200-year time-jump. This, and not the futuristic hardware that Allen allows himself as comedy props, is the real inspiration of *Sleeper.* The security blanket of familiar routines and surroundings is snatched away and Allen retreats nostalgically to memories of his failed marriage and the inevitable divorce. ("My wife called me a pervert because I drank our water-bed.")

In *Play It Again, Sam* — the only one of his films that Allen hasn't directed — the whole story is about the adjustment to the trauma of divorce. The miscreant wife has accused Allen of being "one of life's watchers" and has sued on grounds of "insufficient laughter." Allen cannot cope even with the mechanics of the situation. "I'll tell my lawyer to get in touch with your lawyer," says the existing wife. "I don't have a lawyer," Allen replies. "Have him call my doctor."

The growth of Woody Allen's cinema following has been slow but certain. *Sleeper,* a small film with little advance publicity, was one of the surprise commercial successes of 1974. His shy, neurosis-crippled loser is not only a classic underdog, but a recognisable Everyman for a stress-prone world.

Taboos are less often Allen's targets, but in the firecracker *Everything You Wanted To Know About Sex* But Were Afraid To Ask* (literally a rendering of the sex manual!) he manages to take a firm stand against hypocrisy and the coy attitudes towards sex that still linger in comedy. "The film," he said, "contains every idea I have ever had about sex, including a few that led to my divorce." In a series of short episodes he introduces us to frustrated and over-active couples, a wary transvestite, a psychiatrist (Gene Wilder) who develops a consuming passion for a sheep and finally — in an

set inside the body — himself as a parachutist-sperm who doesn't want to come or go.

A surprise addition to the flourishing sub-genre was *Where's Poppa?*. Surprise in that it stemmed from a novel of no excessive blackness; that it was directed by Dick Van Dyke's scriptwriter, Carl Reiner; that it co-starred George Segal and septuagenarian actress Ruth Gordon, lately returned to the screen after a twenty-one year absence. It was probably the most outrageous of the batch because it was rooted in everyday realities, particularly the harsh (Jewish) family one of committing Mother to a Home. As the bachelor son whose lot it has been to look after this malicious vegetable, Segal stammers terribly at the mere approach to the word "Home."

The film opens on his weary attempt to scare her to death by stalking into her bedroom, dressed as a gorilla, and bounding fearfully on her bed. She wakes up, delivers a devastatingly accurate blow to his crotch and chuckles: "Such a good boy, always trying to cheer me up, always teasing your Momma." Later, when she scolds that he "almost scared me to death," Segal is heard to mutter that, " 'almost' doesn't count."

Reiner begins with normality and, as the film starts to revolve faster and faster, he allows the plot threads to whiplash out into bizarre fantasy. Segal has a day dream about a dog eating the wretched mother ("You see, Officer, she'd been shrinking a lot lately"); a group of muggers force Segal's brother (the admirable Ron Leibman) to commit rape in the park, but when the victim turns out to be a decoy policeman Leibman happily accepts a gift of roses and debates making a second date; installing Mother finally in a Home, Segal answers her perpetual question, "Where's Poppa?" by grabbing the nearest inmate and setting him down like a tailor's dummy before her.

Perhaps the humour was too ferocious at the time of its initial release, perhaps its distribution was inadequate, but *Where's Poppa?* (probably the best single example of the new comedy) failed to ignite at the box-office. Now United Artists have sold it to GTO Films who are presently re-marketing it in harness with the amusing *The Groove Tube*.

More conventionally black was *Harold and Maude,* which also starred the irrepressible Ruth Gordon. Bud Cort and she played the title roles, a teenage faker of suicides and an eighty year-old crank. Unfortunately the couple aren't well enough balanced, either in the writing or in the playing. Maude steals all the limelight with her amiable eccentricities: the ritual of oatstraw tea and ginger pie in her railway compartment home ("Excuse

Ruth Gordon in Harold and Maude

the mismatched saucers"); a prized gift thrown in the river ("That way I'll always know where it is"); the frisson when she announces on her eightieth birthday that she has taken an overdose of sleeping tablets because she thinks it's a good age and time to be moving on.

There are inevitable sentimentalities, but any film that dares put these unlikely lovers into bed together is working hard (perhaps a little too hard) at breaking down the barriers. Hal Ashby's direction, while technically adroit, doesn't show the complete empathy that is to be found in Reiner or Brooks.

By now the new comedies were an accepted part of the cinema diet. Whether or not you found them digestible was a matter of individual taste. But, having got over that first hurdle, of public acceptance, people like Mel Brooks could begin to indulge

themselves a little. "Look, nobody *lets* you make a movie," says Brooks. "Nobody comes up and says, 'Here, kid, take three million dollars and go make a film.' You have to fight every inch of the way. When I was a child I would queue for the movies from the moment they opened in the mornings. Round about nine at night, there would be this flashlight in my eyes and a Jewish voice behind it saying, 'Melvin, you gotta *eat*!' Then I'd been shlepped down the aisle and taken home. But I loved those movies, especially the westerns. Heroes like Tom Mix, WS Hart — I would have married any of them."

In the event, Brooks married Anne Bancroft, but the warmth of his affection for the western is amply demonstrated in *Blazing Saddles* (teeth-grindingly sub-titled "Never Give a Saga an Even Break"). Every cliche of the genre is delightfully exploded and stock situations are revitalised by some bizarre casting (a black sheriff in the Gucci-dressed person of Cleavon Little; Gene Wilder as the alcoholic Waco Kid). Although it is a series of jokes in search of a plot, no movie buff can fail to respond to the film's rude vigour.

Brooks summarises the kind of western he set out to satirise. "Focus on a rock. The bad guy rides past, then the good guy, then the sheriff. Focus on a tree. The bad guy rides past, then the good guy, then the sheriff. And so on. The bad guys always wore black gloves and they stretched and fidgeted them all the time. That was because they couldn't act. All day long they would eat beans and drink coffee with never so much as a burp. And when I allowed a tiny degree of flatulence into *Blazing Saddles,* they said I was vulgar ..." Indeed, Brooks' wind-breaking scene was another screen first.

Most of the criticism of *Blazing Saddles* centred around the narrative laxity. One

American critic described the ending as "sagging like a tenement clothes line." As though in answer to these carps, Brooks provided a firm framework in his horror spoof *Young Frankenstein,* but the fidelity to plot somehow tempered the excesses of inspiration. Nevertheless it was the better film of the two even though the comedy highspots were not so high.

Once again Gene Wilder starred, as the grandson of the infamous Baron, tempted into following in family footsteps and building a Creature (Peter Boyle, touching in the true Karloff tradition) that goes on the rampage. Here the lampoon was of a specific film, James Whale's 1931 *Frankenstein,* rather than of a whole genre, but Brooks worked out some imaginative variations on familiar scenes like the meeting with the small girl and — most hilariously — the encounter with the blind hermit (Gene

Hackman taking refuge under a whiskery make-up). The pace and look of the film were just right and evidently Brooks' stature as a film -maker was growing.

Now, temporarily at least, Wilder and Brooks, two of the major revolutionaries, have gone their separate ways. Wilder has written, directed and starred in his own film (made in Britain) entitled *The Adventure of Sherlock Holmes's Smarter Brother.* "When I started to prepare, it was fun. Then it got busy, then hectic, then frantic. Then it went right over the top," he said just before shooting began. "Once we start filming, I think the worst will be over. All the characters will have been cast, all the props will have been chosen. My assistant and I reckon we can stay home and telephone in the direction. In the evening we will look at the rushes and say, 'Oh, that's good, they did what we told them.' I think the President has the toughest job in the world, then your Prime Minister. After that, it's a close race for third place. France or Italy might be tough, but I think it's me."

For his female lead, Wilder cast Madeline Kahn, undisputed first lady of the new comedy. We first saw her as Ryan O'Neal's impossible fiancee in *What's Up, Doc?* and Peter Bogdanovich subsequently used her less well in *At Long Last Love.* She co-starred with Wilder in his two Brooks films — as Elizabeth in *Young Frankenstein* and, memorably, as the Dietrich-modelled Lili von Shtupp in *Blazing Saddles.*

Brooks' new repertory company comprises himself, Marty Feldman and Dom De Luise. "We're going to be like the Ritz Brothers." In fact, he acknowledges a debt of gratitude and inspiration to the Marx Brothers, from whom all anarchic screen comedy stems. "My favourite film of theirs was *A Night at the Opera,* because it had the strongest story. And that moment when Harpo leaps on the woman with a tiara," he chuckles. "Just to *leap* on her like that. That was mad, that was inspired."

Brooks' new project is entitled *Silent Movie Madness.* "It's a silent movie made in colour in 1975. There's this conglomerate that is going to swallow up a studio. "It's called Engulf & Devour. Their last hope is to make a big, big film and a director reckons that a silent movie might just be the in-thing if they can get names like Robert Redford and Barbra Streisand to appear in it — it's the noisiest silent film ever made.

"I started off my career in colour. *Young Frankenstein* was in black and white. Now I'm making a silent movie. People think that I'm regressing. What next? A still picture — who knows?"

Mel Brooks and Gene Wilder appear together to promote the film Young Frankenstein at the National Film Theatre, London

The Human Face of Science Fiction

Tom Hutchinson

"The trouble with that kind of film for an actor," said Malcolm McDowell, "is the realisation that an audience is going to be far more interested in what the subject-matter is than might normally be the case. It requires quite a submerging of one's natural vanity to realise that the spotlight may, in fact, be falling on the inanimate things around you, rather than you — the living, breathing actor."

McDowell was talking to me after he had made *A Clockwork Orange* for Stanley Kubrick and it was, I suppose, the inevitable reaction that one might get from any actor worth the salt of his own talent when appearing in science-fiction films: a sense that the gimmicks, the special effects, the hardware, are of far more visual importance than the individual performance.

More so than any other films the medium has been adequate enough as a message in itself.

The human involvement in the technology of astonishment, the apparatus of wonder, as revealed in the science fiction film, would seem to be minimal: a small yardstick necessary only as a means of measuring our own capacity to be identifiably appalled in similar circumstances.

"You had to try to out-act all that weird landscape and those funny flying machines,"

Sir Ralph Richardson told me about his incursion into the H G Wells fantasy *Things To Come*. "Lord, I'm sure I hammed it up like mad. But you had to, you see."

Rod Steiger said he had experienced similar feelings in Jack Smight's version of *The Illustrated Man* by Ray Bradbury. "Acting is always a bit of a fight to convince people that your character is a reality of a kind. It's even more of a battle when what is around you, the situation you may be in, is in itself weird and wonderful. You have even more of a job of convincing people that *you* should be looked at as well."

Boris Karloff was another to realise how difficult a task it was for the actor to come to terms with a story that makes real the unreal and plausible the implausible. He, of course, was the Creature in *Frankenstein*, whose story the science fiction writer Brian A Aldiss, has described as being the first really coherent SF story, although in the Gothic mode.

Said Karloff: "All those sizzling flashing lights in that laboratory trying to upstage you the whole time. It was a real challenge to make an audience want to watch you rather than just the *things* around you."

It is that challenge that most good actors have felt to be the principal reason for participation in films concerning science

105

fiction, known to addicts of the genre as SF because it broadens the scope into Speculative Fiction. And it is a challenge that some actors have not been able to take up with any degree of sustained success. They have succumbed to the hardware, surrendered their personalities to the gimmicks in which they were embedded.

It required an impressively strong talent — such as Karloff's — to make some kind of mark on films whose subject matter was usually so outlandish in the first place that human normality had to be larger than life-size to make an impact.

It is as well here to distinguish between SF and horror films, although the two can merge as with *The Thing From Another World.* Basically, horror films are the impossible, the supernatural, made probable. SF is concerned with the improbable made possible, what one critic has called "dreaming in technologically constructed detail."

Left: Sean Connery takes arms against an alien future in Zardoz. Right: Rod Steiger as Ray Bradbury's The Illustrated Man

Horror films, inevitably, also tend to push their human beings into the background — "You can't go on just screaming all your life," said Barbara Shelley, Britain's Queen Of Horror, before she quit the grisly scene — though an actor has some opportunity, at least, to prove his or her mettle against

forces that are often invisible and therefore, from an acting viewpoint, negligible rivals.

"But there's nothing more disquieting than a machine to act with," said Ralph Richardson, somewhat testily. "Give me animals and children every time."

This reputation for effacing, even reducing to extinction, an actor's presence is, it is my contention, fast becoming — and paradoxically as these films are usually concerned with the future — a thing of the past.

One of the great advantages of SF is that it can be used as a distancing mechanism with which to comment upon the present. The literature has always understood that: it can tell us what we are now in the guise of what is to come. More and more film directors have made that discovery.

And, because such comment inevitably concerns Man himself then men form an integral part of the technological pattern being woven by such directorial dreamers. The actor, therefore, becomes as important as all the special effects; because so many recent films have been concerned with the future's effect on people then the actor has to be specially effective himself.

Kubrick realised this, of course, with *Dr Strangelove,* that comically corrosive glimpse

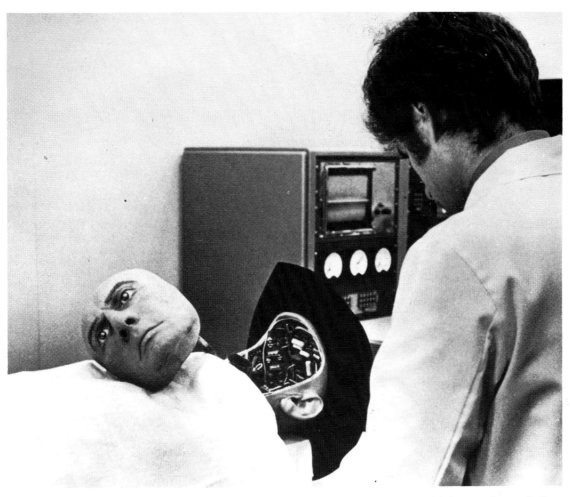

Robot gunslinger Yul Brynner undergoes mechanical repairs in Michael Crichton's Westworld

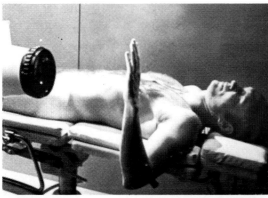

Left, top: James Olson undergoes ultra-violet scanning in the course of Robert Wise's The Andromeda Strain. Left, bottom: man as machine -- George Segal in Mike Hodges' The Terminal Man

of an atomic future, which gave Peter Sellers the opportunity to spread himself around like butter in roles as diverse as the US President (unable to halt a fail-safe device and thus bringing a nuclear holocaust down upon us) and the good Doctor (happily anticipating an underground future, wherein the Final Solution would eventually be reached in the purest of all racial breeding). Sellers was seen here as at one with all the scientific gimmickry; as having an important place in it.

Similarly, with *A Clockwork Orange,* that unsparing look at a future moral Armageddon; mankind is seen as dominating his circumstance, albeit badly. He is in a kind of control which puts us as individuals at the forefront of Kubrick's anger by way of the Anthony Burgess novel.

Where once SF films may have been much more concerned with things that go whirr and clank in the night — rude mechanics to loosen our slack-jawed gasps — they now, like the literature that is its undertow, are as concerned with men as machines. In the case of *The Terminal Man* by Michael Crichton, for instance, with man *as* machine.

This chill indictment of our progress by director Mike Hodges has George Segal as a scientist suffering from a kind of epilepsy; he becomes connected to a computer that is intended to block off his murderous impulses.

Man versus machine in the climax of Steven Spielberg's Duel

The result is that he himself becomes a killing tool.

Crichton's book *The Andromeda Strain,* filmed by Robert Wise, implied similar comment on our inability to control the things which we have made, and he took the idea almost to the ends of its tether with *Westworld,* which he himself directed.

Here we are once more in the future, at a vacation resort peopled by robots meant to look like people and intended to pleasure people in ways ranging from a female robot that can experience orgasm to Gunslinger (Yul Brynner) who is meant to fail at any shoot-out at an oh-yeah Corral.

But here again machines betray us and we don't know why. The Gunslinger runs amok with guns belching lead and death and the result is a bitterly wry comment, not only on our engineered civilisation but, in fact, on our attitude to Western films themselves.

SF films have never been backward at coming forward to warn us about ourselves. *Planet Of The Apes* — I refer to the first one, before the idea decayed into something only

fit for monkey-mask merchandising and TV soap-opera — was a parable which showed us a time-slipped space traveller (Charlton Heston) reaching a planet which is ruled by simians, only to discover that the planet is earth itself after the human race had gone nuclear fishin'.

Heston would seem to have enjoyed that SF experience, since he has made two more warning films: *The Omega Man* and *Soylent Green.* Both were concerned with ecological disaster.

The Omega Man was about a Gadarene world in which all attempts at ethical sanity had collapsed, while *Soylent Green* posited our future planet as a place on which people were pulped back into food after voluntary euthanasia: this last film is even more memorable for the wonderful performance of Edward G. Robinson as an old man opting for suicide.

It is enough, now, that I can remember not only the situations related in these films but such portrayals. The actor has come into his SF own, even in such a misguided attempt as John Boorman's *Zardoz,* made only significant by the dynamism of Sean Connery.

Many of these films, of course, have really reached no further than the warning novels that are already in the genre. But current books themselves have gone beyond wagging fingers of reproach at our infinite possibilities for future bad. And it is good to note that SF cinema itself is going beyond that simple fact of putting on the frighteners.

The man-versus-machine syndrome will always be with us, because of our own subconscious worry about what we have created, but it was refreshing, for example, to see it treated in a different way in *Duel* which had Dennis Weaver as the lone motorist menaced by a giant lorry.

No futuristic gimmicks here, an all-too-possible happening, as anyone whose car has been nearly crushed by an unheeding juggernaut will tell you (me, for one). No wonder Brian Aldiss chose it as his favourite SF film at a recent symposium at the Institute of Contemporary Arts in London. (I chose Hitchcock's *The Birds* which I consider SF because it is about an alien invasion... although from within. Inner Space, as it were).

A vein of poetry has always pumped through all good SF and this was never more apparent than the Russian *Solaris,* adapted from the book by Stanislaw Lem. Its effect is almost impossible to describe, this account of space-settlers who encounter a planet's ocean that can even duplicate memory. There is a feeling to it, that tranced sense one gets with the French director Alain Resnais, concerned with time as he is in *Stavisky* and *Last Year At Marienbad.* There is the same haunting aura of time as a dimension that erodes all we ever do in that other dimension of space... it affects our past as it affects our future.

It is the future that obsesses us in all SF films. And it is a future that we now see populated not only by machines but by people and, therefore, actors: the Human Face of SF has now been displayed in recent years, and I suppose the ultimate deification of humanity comes in Kubrick's *2001: A Space Odyssey* where Man is finally elevated to the status of a god, the Star-Child.

I don't think there's any higher casting than that for an actor.

Charlton Heston, a frequent visitor to the genre, cracking the mysteries of Richard Fleischer's Soylent Green (left) and overpowered by mutant zombies in Boris Sagal's The Omega Man (right)

Funny Ladies

Margaret Hinxman

On consideration the very phrase — "funny lady" — is a contradiction in terms.

A lady is a lady. If she's funny she's no lady. "Witty" is another matter. You can mouth the most devastating wisecracks (as Rosalind Russell and Myrna Loy used to do) and still retain the elegance that fits the Adrian-designed wardrobe and the Sidney Guilaroff hair-style.

But wit flows from the pen of a Hecht or MacArthur or Wilder. It just requires the slight list-to-starboard of verbal delivery that should be as natural to any true actress as high romance or low melodrama.

A funny lady is a very special individual. She commits the unforgiveable crime against her sex: she makes a fool of herself. One of Britain's most gifted comediennes, June Whitfield (who has never been given a chance in the cinema), has a very particular image of the perfect funny lady: Lucille Ball. The secret, as she sees it, is to be gorgeous and funny at the same time. To be able to pull faces, trip over the furniture, fall under the table in a drunken stupor and still look like every man's dream heroine.

I offer no apologies, therefore, in starting this analysis of the ladies who are funny with Carole Lombard. I'll return to Mabel Normand and move on to Barbra Streisand. But I suspect that no actress who tips a toe in the treacherous waters of screen comedy

has not Carole Lombard in mind. In the same way that every actor who tackles light comedy feels the ghost of Rex Harrison and Cary Grant breathing down his neck.

Twenty two years ago in "Sight and Sound," Catherine de la Roche described Carole Lombard as, "the most delicate satirical comedienne the screen has ever had." Bing Crosby, one of her co-stars, summed it up most succinctly: "She had a delicious sense of humour, she was one of the screen's greatest comediennes and in addition she was very beautiful." The last phrase is the vital one. She was very beautiful.

The comedienne treads a dangerous tightrope between farce and humour. She must be able to behave like an idiot and be lovely with it. Carole Lombard had that priceless gift. So, too, did Kay Kendall, although British studios never understood the value of the actress they had under contract. The fact that both actresses died at much the same age, though twenty years apart, is beside the point. They had both established a screen persona that was unique. Lombard, perhaps most memorably as the dotty heroines of *My Man Godfrey* and *Nothing Sacred*: Kendall as the trumpet-playing model in *Genevieve.*

Women can seldom stand up and tell jokes like Bob Hope and Jack Benny. If they do they often fall flat on their faces (ie: Phyllis

*Funny ladies
Greta Garbo
(top left);
Shirley
MacLaine in
Sweet Charity
(top right);
Jean Harlow
with Cary
Grant in Suzy
(below left);
Mae West
(below right)*

Diller). I believe what comediennes must do is to create the ambience of comedy; which is a good deal harder than causing a comic riot in Piccadilly, New York or San Francisco, or fielding the wisecracks of Groucho Marx (like the irreplaceable Margaret Dumont) or Hope and Crosby (Dorothy Lamour).

Neither Lombard nor Kendall were ever stars in their own right (except in the eyes of the public). They simply laid the foundations for their male co-stars — Fredric March, William Powell, Kenneth More — to perform the comic *coup de grace*.

It was not a thankless role but it was a tremendously demanding one and few people outside the profession understood the skill involved in it. The best thing that happened for the funny ladies was the crazy comedy genre of the 1930s. In retrospect it now seems the most sophisticated art that

the cinema, or, more specifically, Hollywood, ever acquired. Every actress of note had to learn the rules — Garbo in *Ninotchka*, Bette Davis in *The Bride Came C O D*.

For years audiences had been conditioned to see actresses in categories. In the silent days there were Mack Sennett's bathing belles and Mabel Normand whose prime skill was slapstick — although Normand was far more talented than a mere knockabout comedienne.

Mary Pickford and Marion Davies injected sly shafts of humour into their roles, but it is only now that filmgoers appreciate the subtlety with which they did it. To the public of their time they were straight heroines, world sweethearts; in Marion Davies's case with the blessing of William Randolph Hearst who himself could never detect the comedienne lurking beneath the glamorous aura he and M G M created.

Marie Dressler was funny. But she was middle-aged and bulky when she became a star: her hero was the equally unprepossessing Wallace Beery. Later Marjorie Main (the splendidly droll "Ma Kettle") carried on the Dressler tradition. And in Britain Margaret Rutherford brought her own special style to the role of the formidable older comedienne.

You could be raucous and funny, like Martha Raye and Judy Canova who kept the jokes coming while the romantic leads agonised their way round some slight detour on the road to a happy ending.

Occasionally, a strident friend-of-the-heroine became a comedienne in her own right. In 1950 Betty Hutton was the hottest star in Hollywood, having schemed to win the title role in *Annie Get Your Gun* after Judy Garland abandoned it — or it abandoned her.

Basically, she was a female Chaplin without that touch of Chaplin finesse. She was all slapstick or all pathos. She couldn't conceive that sometimes 99 per cent is better than 101 per cent in any given scene. After *Annie* her career nodded along comfortably until it faded away through lack of nourishment.

She had had a hard showbusiness upbringing, not unlike Judy Garland's. Her private life was a mess. She agonised over her performances. For Betty Hutton it was no fun being a funny lady. What she did was to bridge the gap between the old conception of a cinema comedienne and the new one as represented by Barbra Streisand.

Carole Lombard, born Jane Peters in 1908, made her first film in 1921. After recovering from a car accident, which incidentally left her with the slight tilt below her right cheekbone that was invaluable in her later comedy portrayals, she worked for Sennett

Goldie Hawn won an Oscar for her first screen performance, in the comedy Cactus Flower

in wretched two-reelers. But she was learning the art of comedy and timing.

Some years later, Lucille Ball (perhaps the most successful, certainly financially, of the funny ladies) learned her craft from Buster Keaton as they consoled each other while sweating out their contracts at M G M.

Carole Lombard went on being nobody very much in nothing very much until she appeared with Miriam Hopkins in *Fast and Loose* in 1931. It was obvious she had the gift for being funny and *soignee* at the same time.

But three years went by before she made *We're Not Dressing* with Bing Crosby. It was a kind of "Admirable Crichton" story and the socialite heroine had to be tatty to prove she was desirable. *My Man Godfrey* in 1936 showed irresistibly that a heroine didn't have to keep her dignity to be glamorous. For Lombard, this led to *True Confession, Nothing Sacred* and, finally, her last film, Lubitsch's *To Be Or Not To Be*.

I have dealt at length with Carole Lombard because I believe every screen comedienne owes a debt to her. Each Streisand comedy is in effect a tribute to Lombard, especially Peter Bogdanovich's *What's Up, Doc?*

During the 1930s, the sedate Irene Dunne cut loose in *The Awful Truth* and *Theodora Goes Wild*. The serious Katharine Hepburn was clownishly inspired in *Bringing Up Baby*. Claudette Colbert allowed herself to be sent up rotten in *It Happened One Night*.

Myrna Loy traded wisecrack for wisecrack, martini for martini, with "Thin Man" hero William Powell and Rosalind Russell had a knock-out comic fight with Paulette Goddard in *The Women*.

In Britain Cicely Courtneidge and Gracie Fields were funny in the broad tradition of English music hall. But in his thrillers, particularly *The 39 Steps*, Hitchcock turned the prim English rose, Madeleine Carroll, into a figure of fun, handcuffed to a man on the run.

While Lubitsch and the censor-bound directors of the 1930s suggested the sin behind the humour, another kind of comedienne was emerging who didn't give too much of a damn what the censor thought: Mae West. She was the quintessential sex-comedienne: the amply endowed woman who made a joke of what she did best — seducing every available male.

"Peel me a grape, Beulah" and "Come up and see me some time" are phrases that should be incorporated in Webster's Dictionary as an illustration of how you can duck the code and Mrs Whitehouse and still sound more erotic than the unexpurgated version

of the *Arabian Nights*. No-one, least of all Mae, wanted her to strip down to reveal all. Fully clothed and upholstered, Mae told the whole story with a nod and an inflection in the voice. Jean Harlow, who was prettier and more indebted to the Hollywood star system (Mae, a star long before she went to Hollywood, was always a maverick) suggested the same sexy style of comedy.

In Britain, Diana Dors came closest to the Hollywood ideal of a sexy funny lady. But it was Marilyn Monroe who, through her lonely, lost, instinctive ability, united the elegance of Lombard, the gutsiness of Mae West and the pathos of Betty Hutton at her best.

In the deeply depressing post-war years, Judy Holliday shone briefly in the Columbia comedies, having created the dim but not so dumb heroine of *Born Yesterday*. Shirley MacLaine is an American facsimile of Guilietta Masina, the female Pagliacci. It is no coincidence that the former starred in *Sweet Charity*, the musical version of Masina's most considerable Italian success, *Nights of Cabiria*.

Some bright American actresses have carved a niche for themselves in screen comedy — Goldie Hawn, Paula Prentiss, Brenda Vaccaro. And no-one is more astute in the art of being funny than Barbra Streisand. The fact that she portrayed comedienne Fanny Brice in *Funny Girl* and *Funny Lady* may be misleading. In fact her most adroit comedy performances have been in *The Owl and the Pussycat, What's Up, Doc?* and moments in *The Way We Were*.

But comedy, like every other style of entertainment, is subject to change. It reflects the mood of the times. The most agreeable of today's funny ladies is Madeline Kahn who can change pace from the game hooker in *Paper Moon* to the seductress of sorts in *Young Frankenstein*. In *Blazing Saddles* she gave a wickedly accurate impersonation of Marlene Dietrich. She is, above all, an actress and you feel she could, given the chance, play Lady Macbeth as well as she tripped the light fantastic in *At Long Last Love*.

Few male comedians are in themselves either happy or funny people. But comedy is a particularly punishing craft for women. The history of screen comediennes is littered with the debris of dead marriages, dead careers and, even, dead people.

"Make 'em Laugh" sang Donald O'Connor memorably in *Singin' In The Rain*. But, even in the world of Women's Lib, it's easier for a man. While a funny man can still be a hero, a funny lady is — a funny lady.

Such Interesting People....

David Castell

There is a *cliché* with which movie journalists learn to live: "You must meet such interesting people." In the cinema, as in any field, one meets rogues, charlatans, outright bores. But if you love movies, even these have their fascination. And, yes, there are interesting people. There are also the people one would have traded a day of one's life to have met—actors, actresses, directors who have become living legends.

Almost invariably they are the elder statesmen of the medium, for length of service lends depth and texture to their memories. Choosing an arbitrary number is a thankless task. The following is not a Ten Best: the omissions are too notable. The selection is highly personal, the order strictly alphabetical. These are some of the people, meetings with whom one approached and left with equal awe. To me they were, are and always will be special.

Dirk Bogarde because he worked unstintingly within the strictures of the British contract system and became a great actor long before we believed the evidence of our own eyes. Olivia de Havilland because of the selfless vigour with which this quiet, elegant actress fought the tyrannies of the American studio contract system.

The terse and taciturn Kirk Douglas because he is a man who has time and again put his reputation on the line for what he believed to be right. Ruth Gordon and Helen Hayes in an unbreakable tie as the screen's most distinguished and experienced actresses. Alfred Hitchcock because he is first and last a moviemaker and thereby has done more than any living man to get the director's name above the title.

Angela Lansbury because she always swam against the tide and finally her perseverance paid off. Paul Newman because he was the first true superstar of the new American cinema and because he demonstrated his belief, through his performances and his sensitive direction, that being Hollywood's blue-eyed boy wasn't in itself enough.

Gregory Peck for being the kind of actor who allowed his gentle personality and liberal politics quietly to influence the films he made and the mark he left on them. James Stewart just for being James Stewart —there are a thousand other reasons but that one is enough.

There is another *cliché*, that a prophet is without honour in his own time. If today's cinema has altered, grown more mature, then it is due in no small measure to the often pioneering work of people like these. To say that they will be remembered long beyond their own lifetimes is no eulogy of idle sentiment. It is an unarguable fact.

Above: Dirk Bogarde in The Serpent. Left: in Hunted

DIRK BOGARDE

Few people took it seriously when, after the launch of *Death in Venice* and palpably at the peak of his abilities, Dirk Bogarde quietly announced that he had given up. He had been, for more than twenty years, the kind of actor to whom people refer as a pillar of the British cinema. Nobody really reflected that pillars have a tendency to hold things up: nobody had bothered to wonder what might happen if the pillar was removed. Since 1948 when Wessex Productions gambled on him as the young male lead in *Esther Waters*, Dirk Bogarde had appeared on our screens (four times as Simon Sparrow alone in the popular series spawned by *Doctor in the House*) with the predictability of a calendar, but none of the monotony. Through the '60s he had shown a new determination and accomplishment, not easily achieved by a contract artist, that culminated in Visconti's invitation to play first in *The Damned* and then in *Death in Venice*.

Today Bogarde has exiled himself to the Maritime Alps where he lives in a French provincial-styled shepherd's cottage which has been converted and developed. It is set into the hills a few kilometres from Grasse and terraced grounds burgeoning with olive trees slope down to the Mediterranean bay between Nice and Cannes. The exile is quite solitary. The proximity of Cannes and its festival deters rather than attracts him. His nearest neighbour (by chance Richard Attenborough, star of his first British film, *Dancing With Crime*, and

117

director of his last, *Oh! What a Lovely War*) is half a mile away.

Sometimes Bogarde wanders into the town to shop in the supermarket. The Europeans, he finds, have a tacit respect for their actors. The fan idolatry that attended his Rank grooming is well into the past. The French refer to him by his surname alone "Bogarde." It is very dramatic. The Italians nod respectfully to him in the street and call him "Il Dottore."

Recently he broke the silence to make two films—the spy thriller *The Serpent* for Henri Verneuil and the controversial drama *The Night Porter* for Liliana Cavani. Does this signal a return to films? "I didn't retire, I just came to a full stop. After *Death in Venice* I said 'that's it.' I won't do anything more for gain, I don't want any more of this two or three films a year lark. It's potty to say that I have retired altogether but I've certainly retired from the rat race.

"Surprisingly I don't really miss anything. Just now and again, when I see someone starting out, I have a certain wistful nostalgia and wish that I had it all to do again. Much of it was very uncomfortable, but I liked it. There's a book to be written . . .

"I always did my very best for the British cinema. And what's more I was aware of doing so from the very early days." False modesty is not an accusation that could be levelled against Bogarde: nor is false respect. He is bluntly, brutally frank in his criticism of his own work and those who have worked alongside him. On the other side he has a clear appreciation of the performances that have been of value and of merit. When Margaret Hinxman and Susan d'Arcy wrote "The Films of Dirk Bogarde"

(LSP, £4.95) the actor said: "I am very flattered, very sheepish and faintly embarrassed. It's like reading your own obituary while you're still alive."

Bogarde learned his film craft during a long-term contract with The Rank Organisation ("Fortunately I had a clause that said I could always return to the theatre." That way he was able to break up the sentence). He says ungrudgingly: "Rank was my university, but eighteen years is a long time to spend with a family. But I was guaranteed x pounds a year to make x films. It was a matter of learning, of fighting, of surviving. The main body of my work there was very silly—I was always critical of it at the time, but nobody understood—but then I never had any illusions. It wasn't as though I had been working in a petrol station or behind the counter in Woolworth's. I was trained in the theatre, so I was very critical from the first."

The Rank films were, for the most part, journeyman efforts that enhanced a kind of domestic star glamour that only Bogarde, among his contemporaries at the studio, possessed. When Hollywood invited him to play Franz Liszt in Columbia's *Song Without End*, it looked as though international adulation would inevitably follow in its wake. The critics were kind, but Bogarde insists that it was a fiasco and he never again returned to film in America. There followed two major events—the thriller *Victim* and the associations with Joseph Losey (they had previously made *The Sleeping Tiger* together in that post-Black List period when Losey had still to operate under the pseudonum of Victor Hanbury).

Victim was about the law that laid homosexuals open to blackmail and the film, though controversial, was actually instrumental in the subsequent homosexual law reform. "It took a lot of courage at that time and you must hand it to Rank for making it. The climate was very different then. I always remember there was a lawyer at the studio whose job it was to read all the scripts, to check that there was nothing actionable in them. When he had read this, he said there was nothing litigatious but that it made him want to go away and clean his hands and wash his mouth out. That was just ten years ago." It also had a dramatic effect on his career. It split the fan image open at the seams.

"The kids just fell away overnight like grass," he said. "It wasn't because I was playing a homosexual, because in England the word 'queer' usually means you're not feeling well, so they didn't get it anyway. But I did have grey temples and I was broaching my own age, playing a man of forty-five. I wasn't the bouncy, happy doctor with a little perm in the front lock of my hair and my caps in and my left profile—every set was built for my left profile. Nobody ever saw the right side of my face in something like thirty films. I was the Loretta Young of England. And so all that broke. The caps came out, the hair was never permed again and a whole new audience came."

The Losey films—*The Servant, King and Country, Modesty Blaise* and *Accident*—took Bogarde further and further away from the stereotype of the Rank days. It also prepared the path to Visconti. Characteristically he and Losey disagree in their choice of favourites. Losey plumps for *King and Country*. Says Bogarde: "I think that *King and Country* and *The Servant* will outlast the cinema itself, but I would most like to be remembered for *Accident*. I think that contains the best of Pinter, the best of Losey and the best of me. But I suppose it is *Death in Venice* that I will really be remembered for."

Contract freedom didn't mean immediate benisons for Bogarde. After the stimulus of working with Losey four times in quite rapid succession, he went into Jack Clayton's uneven *Our Mother's House*, then the only two films he ever hated making—*Sebastian* ("I was so unhappy and disenchanted that I kept my shirt on in one of the bed scenes") and *The Fixer* ("I stuck as closely as possible to the Malamud lines, it was the best any of us could do"). There followed George Cukor's bedevilled *Justine*. After the Visconti experiences there was a tentative plan for Bogarde to work with Alain Resnais in a film about the Marquis de Sade. "It wasn't going to be silly with a lot of leaping about, but a very intellectual, grown-up film. But being Alain, and being me, and seeing that it was going to cost two hundred thousand billion dollars and there was only me in it, it never got made. It still might one day."

It was *The Serpent* that coaxed him out of his semi-retirement. "Henri Verneuil was the first French director, apart from Alain, who had asked me to work for him. He was immensely persuasive and there was the added incentive of working with Henry Fonda. What's more, it was only five days work and they had offered me a knee-buckling amount of money. It had been three years since I had made a film and *The Night Porter* was coming up and, to be honest, I really had lost my nerve and forgotten about camera angles and things like that. It was really all one mammoth dress rehearsal for *The Night Porter*."

Liliana Cavani's film is about the night porter in a small Viennese hotel, an ex-Nazi who rekindles an affair he had with a young girl in a concentration camp during the war. It has aroused controversy wherever it has been shown and was prosecuted in Italy on a "corruption of youth" charge. The film was cleared. "But it made Liliana feel like a dirty woman, it made us all feel dirty. Italy is full of Mary Whiteheads or whatever they're called. Yet the film is a colossal success here in France. One of the major women's magazines voted it their film of the month, and that's a readers' vote where the ages would range from sixteen to seventy-five.

"I'm glad *The Night Porter* was shown in England, and not in that awful general release context where it just wouldn't have been understood. I think it's terribly healthy that all these 600 and 700-seater cinemas are flourishing. The English have always been very pig-headed about the cinema, but the recent changes are very healthy. They nearly came too late for some of us: they *were* too late for some.

"Liliana has another project but it's not exactly packed full of laughs so she might like to leave it for a while. I am going into what the French call *le troisième age*, but of course I will work again. Ten acres of land cost more to support than I had realised. I work all day scything the fields. Someone has to do it if the sheep don't eat up, and this year the bastards didn't turn up."

OLIVIA de HAVILLAND

"Coincidence is not permitted in drama," said Miss de Havilland reflectively, "yet it is happening all the time in real life and it has played an important part in my career."

It was a series of coincidences that brought her to the public eye more than thirty-five years ago. As a

Olivia de Havilland attacks James Caan in Lady in a Cage

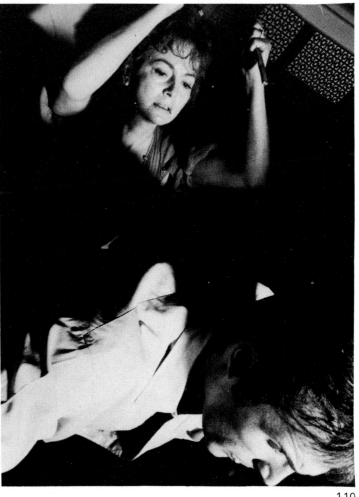

teenager she had committed her life to Shakespeare though, at that time, her service was to be conducted in a local amateur dramatic society. Then she heard that the great Max Reinhardt was to produce "A Midsummer Night's Dream" at the Hollywood Bowl. Via a chain of friends and acquaintances she won an invitation to sit in on the rehearsals, and imagined herself taking the direction by proxy from Reinhardt. By a chance meeting, she won the job as a second understudy and then, with the heavy hand of coincidence taking over, the first understudy got an offer to make movies and walked out. Olivia de Havilland was promoted. The star was herself engaged on a film and, quite unexpectedly, the production ran over schedule and she cabled that she would be unable to make the opening night.

Olivia de Havilland was promoted once more, which is how an unknown girl of eighteen came to walk out on stage at the Hollywood Bowl in front of an audience of 26,000 people including Bette Davis, Joan Crawford and all the major names of the day. "After that," she says, "I was even more dedicated to Shakespeare and was convinced that my career lay on the stage, but Max Reinhardt was going to make the film of the production—he dictated the mood of the film and William Dieterle did the mechanical direction. They wanted me to be in it, so of course I said yes. I had been offered the part of Tina in 'The Old Maid' on Broadway by then. I knew that it was a part that I could do well and which would get me attention and good notices. So this was to be my first and last film . . ."

Warner Brothers had different ideas. They needed a romantic heroine and told the young Olivia that she could only play in A Midsummer Night's Dream if she signed the standard five-year contract. "No contract, no film—that was their deal. They knew how much I wanted to work with Reinhardt again, but I wasn't going to commit my life to something as trivial as movies. I said no.

"But then came another coincidence. I was leaving the casting office and walking through the front lobby when I saw coming through the revolving doors, one behind another, Reinhardt, Henry Blanke the producer and William Dieterle. I felt I had to go over to Herr Professor Doktor, as we used to call him, to tell him what had happened and to thank him for the opportunity he had given me. No sooner had I finished my story than all three men became very excited and began to gesticulate and shout at me in German. There were many 'Gott im Himmels' and they literally backed me into the casting office where I signed. Then I went home and cried till train time.

"It was psychologically dislocating to have one's name in lights suddenly at the age of eighteen. The loss of anonymity was abrupt and total and, at that age, one could not cope with the mass of publicity and interviews. It still startles me today, but then it was overwhelming. I should have refused the contract and gone into the theatre. The loss of anonymity would still have happened but it would have been more gradual, less of a wrench. Even at the time I knew that that path was psychologically sounder."

Today Miss de Havilland surveys her career with a mixture of pride and amusement. She is helped by the gift of total recall and becomes impatient with her memory if it fails to yield instantly the required data—the exact colour of a dress, a precise date, the details of a menu. She recalls a lunch-break at the studio. "I went into the Green Room, sat at my usual table and opened a book. I ate lamb chops with mint sauce, green peas and a baked apple. Just

before half past one . . ." and she goes on to detail a meeting of no specific significance to her. The year, 1936.

She was the great white hope of Warner Brothers and was sometimes referred to in just those terms. Having acquired their valuable property, the studio set out to get their money's worth. In the first year, she made five films, working a six-day week and starting in the make-up department at 6 am every morning. Sunday was a day of total exhaustion. In the early years she met and harboured a crush on Errol Flynn: she was Maid Marian to his Robin Hood.

"The first time I ever saw Errol was on the ramp of a deserted set. We were both very young and I asked him what he wanted most. He said success. He asked me the same question and I answered respect. I always had the feeling that success wouldn't be enough for him, and it wasn't. All that time he never knew that I had a crush on him and, some years later, he got one on me. I sometimes wish that I had spoken out. No I don't. He would have probably ruined my life . . ."

She wrote a letter to Flynn after seeing *The Adventures of Robin Hood* re-issued at a first run cinema in Paris. It was the first time she had realised what a good film it was and wanted to share her discovery with her co-star. But she dismissed the letter as sentimental and never sent it. Months later he was dead.

Bette Davis, a contemporary and close friend ("You don't gain Bette's friendship, you win it"), once said that at MGM they treated stars like royalty and at Warners they treated them like factory hands. It was the lot of Miss de Havilland to be stuck at Warners and, as she followed the example of the better actresses there in demanding more worthwhile and less demeaning parts, it looked as though she might be there for the rest of her working life.

If an actress refused to play a part for which her studio thought her suitable, she could be put on suspension for as long as it took the studio to re-cast and make the film. During this time the actress would receive no salary and could not accept any other offers of work. Furthermore, suspension time could be added on to the end of a contract so that, theoretically, one could be contracted to the same studio for life. Miss de Havilland insists that the stories of her clashes with the studios have been exaggerated. "I never refused to do a film. I sometimes declined, though. I had been at the studio for four years to the day when I first declined a part. I had been getting all my best roles while on loan to other studios. Jack Warner was furious and immediately sent me a telegram forbidding me to go to the Atlanta premiere of *Gone With the Wind* which, needless to say, I ignored.

"I had begged him to let me play the part in the first place and he had taken a long time to agree because he had said I would be impossible when I came back. So this was just the ammunition he was looking for."

When relations with the studio became too strained, she took the matter to court, quoting an old law that said that no contract of employment could be stretched beyond seven years. She put 12,000 dollars of her own money into the fight and was unemployable for the two years that the courts debated whether or not to uphold the first decision (in her favour) against appeals by the studio lawyers. The risk was enormous. Even if she won the case, would any studio risk hiring such a potential 'troublemaker'?

Finally she received the news that she had won. Her greatest pride is that, to this day, that decision is still referred to in legal circles as "the de Havilland decision."

"It seemed to me a most important thing to have done," she says. "The more so since the war was on at the time and a whole group of young actors had gone off to fight. Normally they would have come back after four years in the war to find that their contracts still had a further six years to run. This way they would only have two years, after which they could negotiate a new deal at post-war prices."

Luckily she was offered the better roles for which she had fought and won her first Oscar in 1949 for *The Heiress*, a property that was particularly dear to her. The lack of intensity in her career during the '50s she attributes to the birth of her son. "Until then I had had a single heart and it is remarkable what a single heart can achieve. Suddenly my heart was divided." She has always striven, with notable success, to keep her private and professional lives apart. Even now, living in semi-retirement in Paris, she is unhappy with the idea of working in France, because it is the place that means home to her.

"After the birth of my son, I never put quite the same concentration of effort into my career again. I came back to Hollywood in 1952 from the Broadway stage to make *My Cousin Rachel*. I was aware of the first crash even then. I had a sense of a world already belonging to the past, and belonging to it with increasing rapidity. The whole temper had changed, it was a depressed community. It was a very unwholesome atmosphere for a creative person and so dispiriting to watch a civilisation you had loved sliding into the past. I left immediately and I have never wanted to go back."

Even now, Miss de Havilland thinks with some warmth and affection of the old contract system she helped to beat down. "It had a lot of advantages as well. One learned a lot of discipline and had discipline imposed on you. You also had very little time for rehearsal, so you learned the value of preparation. Most important of all, you learned that second best wasn't good enough."

KIRK DOUGLAS

For many years Kirk Douglas has enjoyed (or at least cultivated) a professional reputation as a tyrant and a hard task master and a private reputation as a hell-raiser. "Virtue isn't photogenic." He has said it in so many interviews that the words will probably be engraved on his tombstone. But possibly he takes this image from his upbringing (school of hard knocks for immigrant boy called Yssur Danielovitch) and the early tough-guy roles he played in films like *Build My Gallows High* and *The Champion*. Prior to coming to Hollywood, his stage success had been only moderate (he was once a stage echo in a Chekhov production where the "Three Sisters" were Ruth Gordon (*q.v.*), Judith Anderson and Katherine Cornell!) and he had promised his mother not only that he would reach the top of his particular tree, but that he would put her name in lights as well. He achieved both ambitions, kept both promises. His production company is called Bryna after her, and he took her to the centre of New York to see an illuminated billboard announcing "The Bryna Company presents . . ."

Kirk Douglas and Deborah Raffin in Jacqueline Susann's Once Is Not Enough

Kirk Douglas portrait, circa 1972

What the company has presented has been an almost constant source of amazement. Douglas was one of the very first actors to form his own independent production company and many expected a mainline stream of fodder within the safe and proven genres that Douglas had already done successfully. Instead, he used the company again and again for experiment, testing and stretching himself as an actor and gaining experience that was to be invaluable later when he took a more and more active part in production.

"I always disliked being *just* an actor," he says. "I don't mean by that that I wanted to become a movie mogul, but it always seemed to me that movies were a collaborative effort. It isn't a medium that depends on one person in the way that a painter can mix his own paints and go on from there. You need a lot of elements, and I was always keen to talk to the producer, the writer, the director. I didn't just want to accept the script and say the lines. I remember that the first time I asked a question on the set, the director turned to me scoffingly and said: 'What's this? A thinking actor?' Now, I tell you, I have more sympathy with the actor than anyone else. Hell, he's the one out there in front of the camera; he's the one whose features are being blown up a hundred times; he's the one that big, cold, impartial eye of the camera is staring at. And I'll tell you, that can be a pretty devastating experience."

Nevertheless that devastating experience got Kirk Douglas to the point where he was in a position to fight back. His survival in those early days came from a refusal to knuckle under and a sincere determination to learn his craft despite the sarcasm and sometimes hostility of those around him. "Now that I produce my own movies, I must admit I sometimes wonder if it isn't better not to bite off so much," (he is not to be believed on this point) "but then the relationship between the people behind the camera and the actor is so unfair in many ways. I remember when we were making *The Vikings*, it was freezing cold and I was darting about bare-chested with very few clothes on trying to pretend it wasn't cold while all the others were wrapped in blankets sipping hot soup to keep warm. It's a small point in itself, but it does illustrate the enormous gap between the two sides of the camera.

"Today entertainment seems to have become a dirty word, but what I hate most of all is pretension. The cinema can make no greater contribution than to make people forget their problems and become lost in what is happening on the screen. You don't go to the cinema to have messages rammed down your throat. If there is a message to be picked up, it must be as a by-product of the entertainment. I get good and tired of the *auteur* system, where the director is God. He's painting with a camera and all that. That's a load of crap. Of course the director is the dominant force, but he doesn't do it *all*.

"I have found that the best directors are the most receptive—people like Billy Wilder and Elia Kazan: they will listen to any idea anyone has to offer. The reason I formed my own company originally wasn't financial—no, really—it was so that I could express myself more. Because of it I was able to pick *Spartacus*, to help with the financing of *Paths of Glory*, to make *Lonely Are the Brave* which the studio would not otherwise have touched. You see, a writer can function with just paper and a typewriter, an artist with just paints and canvas, but to make a film you need a lot of money. My company has given me the muscle to get things done when I would otherwise have been helpless."

Methods of financing in the film industry have changed dramatically even since the Bryna Company has been in existence. "Nowadays there are a lot of extraordinary ways of raising money. With the collapse of so many of the old studios you now have electronics companies and cereal companies making movies. Why, one of my films, it was called *A Gunfight*, was financed by the Indian nation! This particular tribe is exceptionally rich and they have a very sophisticated investment programme and they had heard that I was setting up this picture with Johnny Cash, so they simply rang up and offered to finance it. It sounded like a joke at first."

Co-production is another increasingly popular idea: Douglas remembers the first co-production deal in which he was involved, twenty years ago. It was *Ulysses* and all the actors spoke in their own languages and were dubbed in later. Now he finds that English is the common tongue on *A Man To Respect*, the film he has recently made in Rome.

Although Douglas was never contractually tied to any one studio, he had plenty of time to observe the system at work. It was, he says, making movies by pressing buttons. Everything was too compartmentalised: "I always thought it was wrong that people who didn't make pictures should have the power over the people who did. You either know what you're doing or you don't. It's like being 'a little bit' pregnant."

RUTH GORDON

It may not be gentlemanly to give away a lady's age, but the fact that Ruth Gordon celebrates her seventy-ninth birthday this autumn is a secret too astonishing to keep. This most distinguished American authoress and stage actress has been in and out of movies for more than fifty years. A petite powerhouse of a woman with tremendous reserves of energy, she talks rapidly and enthusiastically about her career—her garden, as she calls it, and the flowers that have grown in it.

Attempting conversation with her is like trying to put up an umbrella in a telephone booth. She rarely gives a direct or concise answer to a question, rather takes it as a licence to roam fascinatingly over the chequered, colourful chapters of her fifty-seven-odd years in the business.

"Do you know what these flowers are?" she asks. It sounds like a quiz, so I say no, expectantly.

"Nor do I. But aren't they the prettiest things? Someone told me they were freesias. I do hope they aren't. I don't like freesias."

A sudden change of subject. "You know, I was at the theatre last night and these two people came up to me and said how much they had loved *Where's Poppa?* They had also seen me in *Harold and Maude*. That's what I miss most over here. At home, all sorts of people come up to me in the street and say they saw me in this play or that film. It's as though the whole world is your neighbour."

In fact, Ruth Gordon is no stranger to Britain. She is the only American actress to have starred with the Old Vic Company. She played in a Restoration comedy and, when she couldn't quite get a bearing on the character, her director advised: "You know Minnie Mouse? Play it like Minnie Mouse—with sex."

This visit is a little confusing as it is the first time she has encountered decimal currency. She has had a tiresome morning, being palmed off with old pennies in a grocery store, quarrelling with the ladies in Fullers (to whose walnut cake she is a slave) over the validity of half-crowns and finally meeting with a distinctly discourteous reception at her bank when she confessed her confusion over the currency.

"I told them I would close my account immediately. When I got back, the bank rang up to say they needed my signature to close the account. I said that was their problem. My signature is worth money."

But such annoyances are rare, as is Miss Gordon's lack of patience with them. "As an actress, I need to think that the whole audience is loving me. It's the only way I can come through. I can't stand to think that there is someone out there valuing me. That's why I would never do screen tests."

She recalls how her husband, Garson Kanin, once asked Somerset Maugham why he hadn't written any more plays. Because he didn't get the ideas any more. Why? Because he didn't *want* to get ideas any more. Ruth Gordon understands that and believes that you can make things happen or not happen as you want.

That's why she was away from the screen for twenty-two years between the 1943 *Edge of Darkness* and *Inside Daisy Clover*: she wasn't offered a part because she didn't want one. She had married Kanin in 1942, played extensively in the theatre, co-written half a dozen screenplays with her husband, written a play of her own and seen her original "Over 21" filmed as *The Actress* with Jean Simmons playing herself when young.

"I didn't enjoy the earlier films," she says of a batch that included *Abe Lincoln in Illinois*, *Dr Ehrlich's Magic Bullet* and Garbo's farewell picture, *Two-Faced Woman*. "I did them for the money and I was never truly happy. But I'm a person who only needs a certain amount of money. When I had enough put away, I stopped."

The calibre of the role of the crazy old mother in *Inside Daisy Clover* sent her off to see producer Alan J Pakula and director Robert Mulligan. "We went to see Natalie Wood, because she had cast approval, and she nodded her pretty little head. We got on just fine. She gave me this."

She singles out a charm on a gold bracelet. It is shaped like a clover. "It said, 'With all Daisy's and all my love.' The engraving has nearly all worn away now, but it's nice to know that the love is still there." Another charm is in the form of a miniature gold Oscar. "Greg Peck gave me that one." Ruth Gordon won her full-scale Oscar for *Rosemary's Baby*. A third charm is of the baby itself, a little gold demon with a tail and flashing ruby eyes. "Mia Farrow gave it to me because you never got to see the baby in the film. He's a real little devil, isn't he? Keeps catching on everything . . ."

Since her return to the screen ten years ago, Ruth Gordon has been bitten by the movie bug. *The Loved One, Lord Love a Duck* and *Whatever Happened to Aunt Alice?* are among the titles, but she saves her special affection for *Rosemary's Baby*. "Roman Polanski is an incredible director. Once he and Mia took a helicopter and went to see Disneyland just while the shot was being set up."

She is also inordinately fond of her two black comedies, *Where's Poppa?* and *Harold and Maude*. "*Where's Poppa?* is a cult film in the States. You rarely find anyone who has seen it once. They have all seen it two, three times maybe. When we were celebrating our thirtieth wedding anniversary, the manager came over to thank us for staying at his hotel. He added: 'By the way, Miss Gordon, I saw *Where's Poppa?* for the seventh time last night.' Garson said: 'Jesus Christ, I thought I was a movie buff, but I've never seen a film seven times, not even my own!' But that's the way it is with that film, and with *Harold and Maude*."

In *Harold and Maude* she plays a gloriously eccentric eighty-year-old whose great gift for life helps bring out a shy, rejected and neurotic young man. Observing her laughing and talking with complete strangers one day, he remarks: 'You sure have a way with people.' She counters with a reply that has as much of Ruth Gordon in it as it does of Maude:

"Sure, they're my species."

Top: Helen Hayes in One of Our Dinosaurs Is Missing

Bottom: Ruth Gordon in Harold and Maude

HELEN HAYES

They call Helen Hayes "the first lady of the American theatre" and you don't need to have seen a single one of her stage performances to realise why. She is the true doyenne, able to look back over a career that is only eight years younger than herself at a vivacious seventy-four. A Broadway theatre is named in her honour and she has received almost as many awards as she has given performances. Sadly, her forays into the cinema have been few. Nevertheless she has won two Oscars, thirty-eight years apart, for *The Sin of Madelon Claudet* and *Airport*, of which latter part she is able to say with disarming honesty: "The minute I read the script I knew which character was going to steal the film." Recently she cropped up as the owner of the enchanted Volkswagen in Disney's *Herbie Rides Again*. Currently she is to be seen in the same company's comedy *One of Our Dinosaurs Is Missing*.

Lunch with the lady, listening to her reminiscences, is like coming across a rare edition of a cherished book. Not that Miss Hayes is one to dwell willingly on the past. The present, one senses, is her favourite tense—with the future a close second. She occupies an impossible amount of space for one so frail and tiny, the hallmark of a true star. She is daunting in her energy and exhausting in her enthusiasms.

This is her third visit to England and her happiest to date. The first two were clouded by the circumstances that governed them. During the war she came over to play in "The Glass Menagerie," under the direction of John Gielgud, a part she took

over on the death of her dear friend Laurette Taylor. "She was a warm and glowing spirit. It was like going to church, the way I adored her, not that I wanted to emulate her. She became very ill during the Broadway run and made me promise that I would do the play in London if anything happened to her. So it was a great responsibility and I was as taut as a bow the whole time."

The second occasion was soon after the death of her husband, the celebrated playwright, Charles MacArthur. "I had been asked to play in the film *Anastasia* but I knew the part was wrong for me. But when Charlie died, friends persuaded me that I should work. I agreed to make the film and I came

over to the Dorchester with Anita Loos. I remember that, in the middle of the production, I went off to Brighton to talk about a play. Just imagine! I hadn't told a soul where I was going. Anatole Litvak was furious with me and I can't say that I blame him. It was a desperately unhappy time for me, as it is for all women who lose their husbands after long and happy marriages."

Now she is installed in a hotel at Burnham Breeches where Gray is said to have written his celebrated elegy. Miss Hayes leans forward, as though to whisper. "They say," she starts with an air of imminent confidence, "that he wrote it in the room I have. But I think they tell that to all the girls. Anyway, a copy of it hangs in the dining-room, which isn't very cheerful. I don't want reminding that all I have done is for nought." When she is not on call at Pinewood Studios, Miss Hayes walks several miles a day, exploring the English countryside. She discovered and entered an English pub unescorted (an adventure she recounts with some pride) and treasures a little restaurant where she can get toad-in-the-hole and rhubarb crumble, dishes that her English grandmother used to make.

Evenings at her hotel, she makes occasional use of the television set to see "Hawaii Five-O" in which her son, James MacArthur, stars. "I was watching the other night and there was an episode in which he had been responsible for an accidental killing. There was very little dialogue, but he just sat there with such an expression of inner pain that it made me cry. I thought: 'Where did he *learn* such pain?' Someone on the set came up to me the next morning and said: 'We saw your Jim on the television last night and he made us cry.' So it's not just a daft mother talking . . ."

The Disney studio has played an important role in the lives of the MacArthur family. After his debut in *The Young Stranger*, James starred in such Disney films as *The Light in the Forest* and *Swiss Family Robinson*: now Miss Hayes branches out with *Herbie Rides Again* and *One of Our Dinosaurs Is Missing*.

On the set, where she is incarcerated in the stern uniform of a Victorian nanny, Miss Hayes relaxes between takes and jokes with Joan Sims and Natasha Pyne. She complains vigorously that the hilarious conduct of co-star Peter Ustinov is unfairly hard on her make-up.

"I have colossal respect for the Disney professionalism," she says. "To make one Disney film a year would be my idea of heaven. I'm so delighted that *Herbie Rides Again* was such a success. Some friends saw an early preview and they all came out looking at their feet and not talking about it. I thought: 'My God, I'm in a *failure*!' Then, when they didn't release it immediately, that only increased my lack of confidence. That's one of the reasons that I did a series of personal appearances to help promote the film. I don't mind so much being a failure in a successful film, but there has to be success in there *somewhere*."

Success has been Miss Hayes' constant companion since her eager mother propelled her through a stage door at the age of eight. She made a silent film, *The Weavers of Life*, at the age of sixteen and was starring in a stage production, "Babs," when the film came out. "All I remember was slipping out to see it between performances with my mother. The entire audience consisted of two sailors, my mother and I. Half way through, one of the sailors turned to his friend and said: 'This is the rottenest film I've ever seen.' And his friend agreed."

Her movie career struck a note of controversy with the seduction scene in *A Farewell to Arms*. "We didn't know how to refer to the scene," says Miss Hayes, whose co-star was Gary Cooper. "It took place under a statue of a man on a horse, so we called it 'Under the Horse' whenever we talked about it." The Hays Office felt less delicately and excised the scene altogether. Today's screen attitudes horrify Miss Hayes and simple squeamishness keeps her away from the cinema more than she would like. Another point in her case for Disney.

Her love of the cinema is genuine, but her decision to defect to the medium is not entirely voluntary. "It's all that is left to me. I *hate* television and I will never again do a series like 'The Snoop Sisters.' They are just not prepared to spend the money on getting good scripts. And three years ago, doctors told me that I had to give up the theatre.

"It turned out that I was allergic to theatre dust. Funnily enough, a doctor had told me the same thing thirty-five years earlier and we had laughed it off. Charlie said he would put up a tent for me in Central Park! But I would start a play and always I would become ill and have to go into hospital. I never knew how long it would last or when it would happen. The play would close or an understudy would go on. I *hated* being so unprofessional."

Fortuitously, just before the death sentence was pronounced on her stage career, Miss Hayes had made one of her rare screen appearances (her first in thirteen years) as the stowaway in *Airport*. "I really had no thought that I might win an Oscar, otherwise I would have been right there on the evening. As it was, I was appearing in a play at a university theatre. Ros Russell received the award for me—thank *God* she didn't cry—and I watched it on television. The students all came by and serenaded me under the window and we drank their dreadful red wine out of paper cups." A celebration lacking the finesse of the official party, but one more directly to Miss Hayes's tastes.

Although one might imagine it was like asking an athlete to part with a limb, Miss Hayes was not bitter about her enforced retirement from the stage. "The theatre had been getting very odd. It had lost sight of the fact that it was there to entertain, to illuminate. Suddenly everyone was an *artist*. That's a word I would banish from our vocabulary. I have known very few artists in our time. Laurette Taylor was one, Laurence Olivier was another. Me, I'm proud of my *craft*. I worry a lot about the theatre, it has become very wayward. But when the doctors told me that I must give it up if I wanted to hang on to life for a few more years, I had no choice. Hang on? I'd give anything to hang on. I *love* this life."

ALFRED HITCHCOCK

To a meeting with Alfred Hitchcock one carries a burden of preconceptions. It is hard to reconcile the legend of the tyrant director and the macabre geniality of the man behind that perfect semi-circle of a profile. In fact, the two co-exist: amiability and ruthlessness along with a pedigree of finely tempered steel. The frame is larger than one expects, a massive body balanced daintily on tiny feet; the voice is plummier and slower to speak, a voice that attracts but defeats so many imitators.

He has given us fifty-two films in a career that has spanned upwards of forty years in the industry, in silent days and in sound, in England and in Hollywood. His most recent suspense thriller, *Frenzy*, was hailed by some as a return to peak form

Alfred Hitchcock directing a scene in Topaz

He reckons that his fate was sealed (and happily so) by the time he made the first *The Man Who Knew Too Much* in 1934. He was classified in the public mind as a maker of thrillers. He re-made the film twenty-two years later, the only time he has tried a re-make. In retrospect he prefers the first version. "I think it was more spontaneous—it had less logic. Logic is dull: you always lose the bizarre and the spontaneous." Now, of course, the path is set unalterably. "I could never make a musical because the audience would all be waiting for one of the chorus girls to drop dead. A painter always paints variations on the same picture. I plunder my own films for ideas, but in my business self-plagiarism is hailed as style."

Does he feel that some critics, particularly in France, have over-intellectualised his work? (Those who have published monographs and appreciations of his work include directors Claude Chabrol, Francois Truffaut, Jean Douchet, Eric Rohmer, Lindsay Anderson and Peter Bogdanovich). "Maybe," says Hitchcock, "but I'd rather that than the other way around. I remember the terrible panning we got when *Psycho* opened. It was a critical disaster. One critic called it 'a blot on an honourable career' and a couple of years later reviewed Polanski's *Repulsion* by saying it was 'a psychological thriller in the classic style of Hitchcock's *Psycho*.' It's down in black and white for anyone to read." Hitchcock reminds one of the director who claimed that his films went from being failures to being masterpieces without ever being successes. "Perhaps the films are too subtle for them. They seem to take about a year to sink in."

One gathers that, rather than taking a dim view of the British critics, his view is that they are a bit dim. "I knew we were in for a roasting with *Psycho* for two reasons. First, I had insisted that no-one should be admitted after the film has started. People thought this was a gimmick. It wasn't. It was just that the leading lady, Janet Leigh, is killed off very early in the film and I didn't want latecomers wandering in and being distracted wondering when she was going to appear. Second, I insisted that the critics must see the film with an audience.

"I sent a man over from Paris to see to the press showing and to double the advertising budget. I knew Paramount wouldn't take a stand against the critics unless they were prodded. The critics like to see films in privacy and comfort in the mornings and now they were being jostled and elbowed by the paying public. So they called an emergency meeting of the Critics' Circle right there in the foyer of the old Plaza to decide whether or not they were going to stand for it. The Chairman was all for boycotting the film, but in the long run most of them went in and, of course, they hated it. One poor man was so angry that he wrote a letter of protest to the head of Paramount in Hollywood. Of course it was quite useless. I owned the film and just let Paramount have 25 per cent of the profits for putting up the finance."

When *Frenzy* opened (in the modernised Plaza building, ironically enough) the Critics' Circle lunched Hitchcock at a restaurant in London. The lunch was to celebrate the arrival of *Frenzy* and because they felt it might possibly be his last film. Hitchcock demurs. "Retire?" he asks incredulously. "Whatever for, whatever *to*? I should be opposed to any such nonsense. I'm looking for new material at this very moment."

The telephone rings, as though on cue, and it is Tony Shaffer, who wrote the script of *Frenzy* (Hitchcock dismisses the author of the original book as "a man with what I would call a red-faced voice,

at the age of seventy-three. One is tempted to say that he is young for his age, but one can hardly expect a man of these energies and of this intelligence to vegetate just because he has reached pensionable age. Inertia is, after all, its own reward.

Mrs Hitchcock, as tiny as her husband is immense, is darting across the room. "Zip me up, Hitch. It's all right. I'm decent." Hitchcock completes the operation with practised ease and his wife jokes: "If the worst happens, he can always be my maid." It seems eminently unlikely that the worst will happen now: Hitchcock has passed the danger spots in his career (the introduction of sound at Elstree and his experimentation on *Blackmail*, the first British talkie in 1929; the criticised move to America to make *Rebecca* for Selznick eleven years later) and he is now in a position of almost unparalleled power for a film-maker.

He owns most of his films and has absolute artistic control, a clause written into his contract which he himself admits is so powerful that he is scared to invoke it, except under extreme provocation. "I could film the 'phone book if I wanted to" he says, and means it, "just as long as I brought it in under three million dollars. Nobody would raise a finger to stop me."

Today is a sad day for the Hitchcocks. The lunchtime editions have brought news of the death of Margaret Rutherford, a loved colleague, and the evening papers announce the death of Cecil Day-Lewis, the poet laureate, another friend. There is a fidgety, fitting silence and then the lugubrious tones begin: "At the funeral of the great comedian Harry Tait, all the comedians of the day were there as mourners. And there was this younger chap who found himself standing next to old Charles Coburn. 'How old are you, Charlie?' the young fellow asked as they stared down into the grave. 'I'm eighty-nine' said Coburn. 'Hardly seems worth going home, does it?' said the young chap."

Humour has always been an essential part of the Hitchcock thriller and often, as here, it is used to break a mood or punctuate a tense scene. It is also a vital part of the man himself, though Hitchcock admits to some confusion as to where black comedy ends and the macabre begins: he decides that *The Trouble With Harry*, a great favourite, was a comedy (even the scene with Teddy Gwenn dragging the corpse by its legs as though they were the handles of a wheelbarrow and encountered by the widow who merely asks: "Are you having a little trouble, Captain?") but admits as macabre the breaking of rigor mortis-stiff fingers to retrieve an incriminating piece of evidence in *Frenzy*.

very apoplectic"). Hitchcock talks of the film's reception at Cannes and how he took Grace Kelly ("Her Royal Highness or Serene Highness or whatever she calls herself these days") to a viewing. One forgets that he was the unlikely Cupid when his star and *protegée*, filming *To Catch a Thief* in Monaco in 1955, fell in love first with the Principality, then its Prince, in Hollywood's last fairytale.

Hitchcock confesses to pigeonholing ideas against possible use in future films. His rococo delight in the macabre is demonstrated in an idea, as yet unused. "The film opens with a long, long shot of two men walking along having a conversation. In the background is one of the Detroit assembly lines and we see a car being assembled from nothing. As they finish talking, one man opens the door of a newly assembled car and a dead body falls out. Where did it come from?"

But his favourite projected opening scene concerns a prima donna at Covent Garden. "As she throws back her head to hit a really high note, she sees one man move behind another in a box above her. There is a knife, and the note turns to a scream. Now, the audience applaud wildly because it is the highest note she has ever struck, but just then the body falls from the box into the orchestra pit. Pandemonium breaks out. The safety curtain is brought down and backstage the prima donna is almost fainting. She is ushered to her dressing room and she signals all her retinue out. 'I must be alone. Leave me.' Then, as soon as she is alone, she picks up the 'phone and dials a number . . ."

It's no good asking what she says, because Hitchcock just shrugs his shoulders. He hazards a guess: "Fritz, it's all right." He toys with the idea, then discards it. "No, then it would have to be a spy story and they're terribly *passé*."

One remarks that there was some surprise at his two successive previous films—*Torn Curtain* and *Topaz*—being in the espionage genre. "*Topaz* was a most unhappy picture to make. The ending I put on was a duel in a deserted football stadium. But it didn't go down well with audiences, so I changed it. I could have fought the decision, but it didn't seem worthwhile. What worried me most about that film was not the ending, it was the fact that we had Cubans and Frenchmen all speaking English together and understanding one another. It just didn't ring true. It was the same when we had Julie Andrews as a scientist in *Torn Curtain*. It wasn't convincing: every time we came to a scientific line in the script I had to cut it out."

He is particularly proud of two innovations in *Frenzy*—his use of natural sound and a superb suspended camera shot that defies description out of context, but will be remembered vividly by anyone who has seen the film. Sometimes he pulled the volume up to three times the normal for an effect, sometimes drained it all away save one crucial noise. "One has always to try and dodge the cliche" he says. "In *Frenzy* I had a scene where a girl comes back to her office after lunch to find that her employer has been murdered. There was no point in following her up the stairs, cutting to her opening the door, finding the body and then giving a close-up of her screaming. I just left the camera outside the building, static, until the scream came. The audience knew what to expect, so why should I do the work for them?

"What particularly appealed to me about the story was the use of the Covent Garden location. There is the market, there are the potatoes, there is the dust and then there is the clothes brush. They all tie in together in a way I think is essential. An audience must have information if they are to care about the characters. There are too many so-called 'mystery' films today: half the time you don't know who the people are or what they're doing. Nowadays there are too few films and too many photographs of people talking. The essence of a film like *Rear Window* is to keep it all in that one room—make it as claustrophobic as possible.

"I am a purist working in the newest art form of the twentieth century. The business is to put a series of images on the screen. The images create ideas and the ideas create emotions, just as words create sentences. This is where the power of montage is so great. Take two shots of Jimmy Stewart: in the first he looks straight at the camera and in the second we see him smile. Separate them and put in the middle a shot of a woman nursing a baby and, you tell me, what kind of man is he? Right, a nice guy. Now, take away the shot of the woman with the baby and replace it with a shot of a young girl in a bikini. Now he's a dirty old man! That's the power of the cinema. Another thing is that the cinema gives you the unique ability to copy a work of art and exhibit it at the same time all over the world. This is the most exciting thing of all."

The casting of Jon Finch and a group of actors best known for their work on the London stage seemed a brave start for *Frenzy*, the more so since, at the time of casting he couldn't possibly have seen Finch in Polanski's *Macbeth*. "It wasn't really brave" says Hitchcock. "You take an unknown actor. If he doesn't work out, you get rid of him. Musicians are the biggest problem, because you never know what you're buying: they will never give you a sample of the score. Writers can also be a headache: my pet hate is what I call the play-in-the-drawer author who sits with his chin cupped in his hands, staring into space with your script blank on his desk. Then suddenly he has an idea. He picks up a pencil and jots it down—on the play in the drawer which he has been writing on your time and money as well."

Hitchcock's was the only director's name that could be used to sell a film for a long, long time, and he lent it to books, to records and to a television series that has launched several newer directors. He himself controlled the series, introduced the films and personally directed nineteen of them, including his favourite (an hour of film shot in two days) in which Barbara Bel Geddes murders her husband with a frozen leg of lamb and watches the police eat the evidence while puzzling over the nature of the murder weapon.

ANGELA LANSBURY

Angela Lansbury swings first one neatly trousered leg over the arm of her armchair, then the other. Paradoxically she is least at ease when she is still. Conversation with her is punctuated by rounds of Elizabeth Shaw Mint Crisps ("I call them liquid headaches, they're so rich—take them away!") and cups of tea. Her eyes are wide and blue, in an expression of permanent and pleasant surprise. Her jaw is square and firm and with that unmistakable jutting angle that makes one long to know what she really means when she says that, in the early days as a contract artist, she "*prevailed* upon MGM" not to do this and that. Her golden hair is cut in a page-boy style that makes her look like the principal boy in a very special pantomime. If one hadn't fallen in love with her twenty years ago, one certainly would do so this afternoon.

Miss Lansbury has, of course, recently been through a great love affair with the theatre as the star of the Broadway production of "Mame" and then in the London production of "Gypsy," and she admits to adoring, sometimes even needing, the presence of a live audience. Yet it is as a movie actress that she thinks of herself first of all. "Even when I am in the theatre I always find myself using movie techniques," she says.

London-born, Miss Lansbury lived in Hampstead until the war. "I became fascinated by the cinema while I was still a child. From the age of eight, I used to go twice a week, by myself, with my pocket money and my Mars bar. At that time it was only 8d." But although she surrendered hours to the celluloid fantasies of the screen, it was some time before the idea of becoming an actress occurred to her with any seriousness.

"It's a curious thing, you know. I had a make-believe life when I was a child that I would be like the characters in the movies I saw. I lived a kind of secret life in which I was always a character in a story in which I was involved. When I was on 'buses I would stare out of the window and look as though I had T B, always playing someone other than myself. I was deeply involved with whichever character I was playing, and this made life bearable. Fortunately I had a couple of friends who were prepared to play this game along with me.

"I used to think about America a lot, but I never thought of myself as an actress or as playing those roles—I was just going to *become* one of them. I was going to go to America and walk down those golden sidewalks, step into a club, and meet Boston Blackie on the corner. That was my Make-Believe Mountain. But then, of course, the war came and my mother really railroaded me into starting something. She said why didn't I enrol at a school of dramatic art? She was an actress herself and thought I had the right qualities. In any case, she said, it would be a good training and discipline for whatever I ultimately decided to do."

Rehearsed and coached by her mother, she auditioned with the balcony scene from "Romeo and Juliet" and won a scholarship to the Webber Douglas school in London in 1939. But then, as the bombing of London was stepped up, her studies were interrupted by the move to America.

"My mother arranged it all actually. My father had died when I was nine and she had decided that London was going to be blown to smithereens and she would get us out if she could." The Lansburys (mother, Angela and her twin brothers) were evacuated under the sponsorship of an American family and, fortunately, Angela was able to continue her dramatic studies in New York, having won another scholarship through the American Theatre Wing. "So my training was split between London and New York, which wasn't a bad thing at all. I always said that in England you train to go on the stage; in American you train for the stage, the radio and the movies; and in Hollywood you just train to go into the movies."

When success came in the shape of an MGM contract, Miss Lansbury was understandably delighted. She learned quickly how to adapt the techniques from the theatre and was constantly in demand in the late '40s in a series of roles, many of which required her to play characters older than herself.

"The studio rather let me be because I was an odd bird to them. They started off wanting to mould me, change my name, that kind of thing, but we prevailed upon them not to do those things. I certainly didn't fall into any category. My contemporaries at that time were Gloria de Haven, June Allyson, Ann Miller—they were the starlets, the up-and-coming young women of the time, and they were so perfect that I was absolutely awed by them. They were all so cute and they all took a size nine, and I was rather large and acting all over the place. As it turned out they were rather awed by me, because I was heavy stuff. But I envied them enormously—American girls always seem so put-together, with the bobbing hair and that tremendous ease—so I felt terribly untidy and ungroomed. I taught myself everything I did because I couldn't be like them, I didn't know where to begin, yet in a funny sort of way I wanted to be.

"There was a curious sort of social life at the studio. When you were at MGM in those days, my dear, there was a whole scene—the arriving, coming into work, going into make-up department in the mornings, who made you up, who did your hair, where you sat. In other words there was a whole heirarchy, because it wasn't just Gloria de Haven, June Allyson, Ann Miller and I in there— it was *Miss* Greer Garson, *Miss* Katharine Hepburn, *Miss* Joan Crawford. It was all fascinating and glamorous and exciting. MGM was the absolute palace of the studios. It was the best, the cadillac, and we used to hear tales of the other places that were terrifying. But, of course, there came a time when you wanted to get out, and I did, I was loaned out. I went to Paramount and it was like going to a lovely weekend houseparty, it was all so cosy. Metro was a great, expensive factory for movie stars."

There can be little doubt that Metro did their star-making job superbly, or that Miss Lansbury was right in back of them with the dramatic ability that so many of her contemporaries lacked. The dramatic weight of her performances led her into heavier and heavier roles (she still remembers being booed publicly for being hateful to Judy Garland in *The Harvey Girls*). But it wasn't really until the late '50s, as the tiresome society mother in *The Reluctant Debutante*, that her comedy flair was given its full, sophisticated rein. And the '60s brought her two magnificent roles in the Frankenheimer films *The Manchurian Candidate* and *All Fall Down*, and the chance to work three times with her close friend and a favourite director, Delbert Mann, in *The Dark at the Top of the Stairs*, *Dear Heart* and *Woman Without a Face*. This last offered her a tiny part as "a blimp of a woman," but Miss Lansbury's disappointment at not being able to work more fully with a loved director was surely eclipsed by the news that made it impossible. She had won the title role in the musical production of "Mame".

She had already conquered Hollywood: now Broadway was to fall as well.

"Fortunately I never saw Rosalind Russell in the film *Auntie Mame*. I hear and can imagine that she was superb. But I had to be totally myself, totally original. Not having seen Ros, I couldn't follow or copy her: I was really very glad never to have seen that film. People are always saying that I have come out of a lot of different holes in my career and they ask me if I have a favourite. Well, of course, I do, and it's the one people think of you least in connection with. The thing I enjoy most is giving a rather credible dramatic performance in a musical setting, and it was in "Mame" that I came closest to melding the drama and the music. I wish I could have done it in London as well, because some of my most loyal fans are in this country. The people who

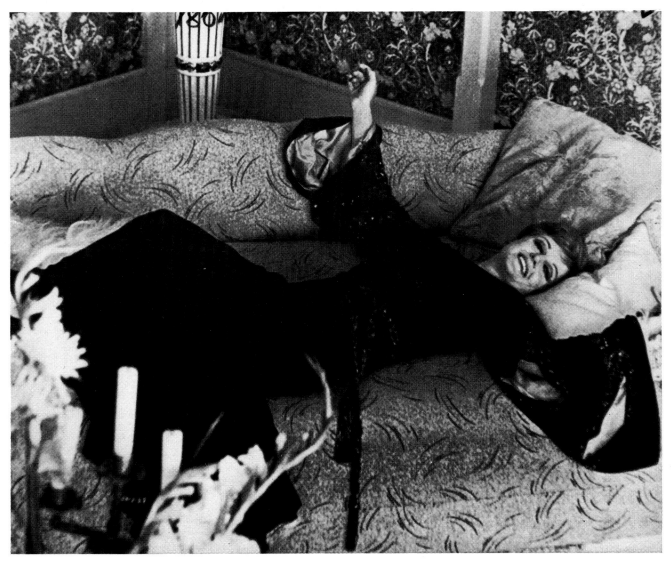

didn't see it the way we did it in New York don't realise what the hell I was doing for those two years on Broadway, because what you saw at Drury Lane was a different show from the one we did. The scenes with the little boy, which are real soap-suds time, had the audience in tears. When you think about Mame herself, it's ridiculous: she's lost all her money in the Crash, and here she is with three servants waiting on her. But the key to the whole thing was that we played it as though it was O'Neill.''

The casting of Angela Lansbury as Mame began a tide of great movie ladies being rediscovered on Broadway: Anne Baxter, Alexis Smith, Lauren Bacall have followed, even Katharine Hepburn in "Coco." But this was a part on which Miss Lansbury had set her heart. ("I couldn't imagine a more perfect way to come on strong with a musical: it was worth fighting for. I'm not usually a fighter when it comes to parts. I have a lot of pride and if they want someone else, I say, Okay, and back down.") She had made her debut in a 1963 stage musical called "Anyone Can Whistle" in which she starred with Lee Remick. It was a satirical look at growing racialism in the South and was severely criticised for straying into the areas of sociology where the musical had no right to be. It lasted exactly nine performances, but all the "Mame" team had seen it on its out-of-town runs, where it had developed a cult following.

Some of them rooted for Lansbury from the very first, but the producers were after bigger fish. They wanted Mary Martin (who was actually signed at one point, but bowed out as she felt she wasn't right for the part after all) or Ethel Merman (who was tired and didn't want to come back to Broadway) and even toyed with the idea of other Hollywood actresses (Lucile Ball—who made the subsequent film version—and Ann Sothern were suggested). But in the long run they capitulated and, after a year's patient waiting, she was given the musical part of the decade.

"Making movies is domestically more convenient," she says, "but the theatre is the place for exuberance and sheer excitement. Every night a different audience: every night you have to go out and get them. I don't change a performance much once I have set it. Some nights I may go a little further, some nights the audience may demand more—that's all. The best part of a long run is after about three months when you have settled in and realised how easy it seems, and the audience is like a bit of putty in your hands.

"I devoted two whole years of my life to 'Mame,' by which I mean that I spent the whole day preparing for that 8.30 curtain. I had to rest, I had to have an afternoon sleep, there were certain things I could and could not eat. It was a very special and rarified kind of life. But the rewards were enormous. It was like everything you have ever read—the front table at Sardi's, like living on an altogether different planet. Everyone loves you, everyone loves the success and enjoys it as much as they hope you do. And it lasts as long as you are on that stage and as long as you keep on coming out of that stage door. I know that I am Mame forever to a

Angela Lansbury as the decadent Countess in Black Flowers for the Bride

lot of people: I'm part of their furniture. They say, 'That was really it, girl, you really had it then.' They don't want you to do anything else and burst their bubble."

In fact, when she left "Mame", Miss Lansbury went into another musical called "Dear World," based on "The Madwoman of Chaillot." "I played a seventy-five year old woman. On the whole the critics were very polite, but the audiences went away disappointed. It only ran for six months."

Her stage ventures have robbed the movies of Miss Lansbury's talents for rather a long time now. Recently she has made two appearances, as the decadent Countess in *Black Flowers for the Bride*, and as the amateur witch, Eglantine Price, in Walt Disney's *Bedknobs and Broomsticks*. On the latter film she particularly enjoyed the sequences in which she appeared with cartoon characters. These were shot against black velvet, and the animated figures drawn in much later. "It was a fascinating thing to have done," she says, "because Disney does that kind of family musical so well and it will be nice to think of the film introducing Angela Lansbury to a lot of youngsters who would otherwise never have heard of her."

PAUL NEWMAN

Paul Newman has it spot on. "If there's one thing more boring than talking about yourself," he says as he is handed a mountain of press cuttings that resulted from his visit to England to star in the thriller *The Mackintosh Man* for John Huston, "it's reading about yourself." There were massive articles on this charismatic actor who, as the '60s nudged into the '70s, was unarguably the world's top box-office star. All warned of the problems incumbent upon meeting Newman: he was elusive, he was not one to open up or communicate freely. Ultimately one was prepared for someone humourless, inarticulate and monosyllabic. Whatever the impression he gives on home soil, here in the more relaxed atmosphere of a Huston-London working environment, he gave the solid lie to all three claims on his behalf. He has a quick, infectious sense of humour; he waxes eloquent on subjects that engage his grasshopper attention. The only drawback is perhaps the rhythm of his speech which is at first difficult to catch: he pauses for the longest time, eyes seemingly focused on some point in the mid-distance, until the most relaxed of inquisitors could be pardoned for thinking his chain of thought complete. Suddenly drumming fingers (on his lips, on the table, on his forehead) will announce that the connection is still live and he will snatch a word from the air to continue the sentence.

Newman appears from an office in a modern production block at Pinewood—taller, leaner than one had expected, wearing a blue-striped shirt with a blood stain on the collar and a ridiculously short tie. His grey hair is worn very short and he is patently fit. As one watches him for any length of time—compulsively crunching Melba toast in a restaurant, downing lager from the bottle neck, taking handfuls of salted popcorn from a red-lidded saucepan in his office—one marvels that he remains so trim and wiry in middle-age (he has now turned fifty).

Departure for lunch is delayed a little: a production secretary is trying to convince Paul that one of the stills from *The Mackintosh Man* is an ideal replacement for a rather out-of-date official fan club portrait. Newman demurs at first. He isn't too fond of the lines beneath "my baby bloodshots." Next he rings the Berkeley Hotel where he is staying. "I would like to leave a message for Mr Paul Newman. Will you ask him to telephone Mr George Roy Hill in California this evening?" Does Mr Newman know Mr Hill's number? Yes, he does. May the operator say who was calling Mr Newman? Mr Newman. She seems used to this idea of their resident celebrity reminding himself of things to do. And so to lunch. The short car journey is occupied with itinerary queries. Does he want to do anything about Election Night? The satellite people wrote to him. Yes, he got the letter. They gave him two dates, but he's working on both of them. "I think we're in for a surprise from Tricky Dick," he says. "He could just win every state and that would be the first time an American President had done that since George Washington." Newman settles into the restaurant, orders a lager and then another. Then an order of rare steak ("I could eat four of these") and fried onion rings. The patented Newman method of coaxing tomato ketchup out of recalcitrant bottles is duly demonstrated and finally, inevitably, the conversation turns to movies.

The Mackintosh Man is Newman's second successive film for John Huston. The previous one, *The Life and Times of Judge Roy Bean*, was only a limited success. "John is amazing. He just sits there and sucks on that cigar. It's as though it all goes up into his head some place. That cigar is the centre of his creative being. When we were making 'Roy Bean' it was sheer joy to get up in the mornings. I read the script and loved it, but I never thought of it for myself. Then gradually I realised I couldn't let anyone else play it." Paul plays a hanging judge who tames an outlaw town and brings civilisation to one of the wilder corners of the old West. One of his accomplices in this exercise is a bear, bequeathed to him by an old mountain man. "It's really an adult fairy story with other characters threading in and out the way they do in real life. People come and go. Things change. I tell you, I fell in love with that bear: this trip I thought of bringing him over and locking him up in a motel room in Knightsbridge! The trainer also had a lion which he brought to the location. We found that although the bear would only work for food, the lion was capable of genuine affection. It was funny: we would be playing cards in the trailer when the lion would saunter in and suddenly there would be guys climbing up the curtains. I had this line I managed to work into the script when Bean puts Roddy McDowall in the cage with the bear: 'The last time he ate a lawyer, he had the runs for thirty days.' "

Authorship of odd lines in his scripts is one of Newman's regular activities. He claims as his own the dialogue in *Butch Cassidy* when Butch, Etta and the Kid first arrive in Peru. The train draws away to reveal them standing in the middle of a wilderness and Butch says: "To think that just fifty years ago this was nothing." "I spoiled so many takes on that line by laughing. Finally I started to crack up the minute I opened my trailer door." Newman's contribution to the dialogue of *The Mackintosh Man* comes in a scene where he is trying to work out which country he is in. One suggestion is France, another Yugoslavia.

"I hope it's not Yugoslavia," says the Newman character. "Because you can't tear the toilet paper and the money comes apart in your hands."

Newman went to Hollywood twenty years ago. He remembers it vividly and with embarrassment. "I

Above: Paul Newman fights the flames in The Towering Inferno. Below: publicity poses, circa 1954 (left) and 1963 (far left)

went straight into a religious epic called *The Silver Chalice* with Jack Palance, Virginia Mayo and Pier Angeli. The dialogue was unspeakable: 'Oh, Helena! Is it really you? What joy!' I was so ashamed. I thought I was finished." One of the kinder American reviews said that he spoke his lines "with all the passion of a conductor calling out local bus stops." Fortunately Newman's contract allowed him to do plays as well and it was through a Broadway production of "The Desperate Hours" that he regained the respect of his fellow actors—and of himself. Robert Wise's *Somebody Up There Likes Me* put him back on the right tracks cinematically, and it was in this film that he first met up (in a two-line part) with Steve McQueen, now a partner in the First Artists Company and co-star in *The Towering Inferno*. "I hate to play prophet," says Newman, "but I saw his potential right off. I told Bob Wise: 'You keep your eyes on that kid, he's got something.' "

As a film actor, Newman gained more and more respect, but often in projects (like *Cat On a Hot Tin Roof*) for which Warners had only loaned him out. "I got 12,000 dollars for that film. The rest all went to the studio. Finally I bought out my contract. It nearly ruined me, but it was my first step towards freedom."

The '60s were a golden period with some plum parts ("All my best roles have been character parts. *Hud* was perhaps the most misunderstood. He became a kind of hero among the young people") and his first chance to direct a feature, *Rachel, Rachel* (he had previously directed an Anton Chekhov monologue at the New York Actors' Studio). He admits to being drawn to emotions in the material he directs, the rawer the better. "My motto as a director is 'Fuck Cool.' I'd love to have it stencilled on the back of my chair and written on signs in letters a foot high. For my camera I have a one-word motto: 'Eavesdrop.' "

Directors who are popular with Newman the actor include Stuart Rosenberg (*Cool Hand Luke*) and George Roy Hill (*Cassidy*). After Rosenberg's

WUSA, a political thriller that finally drew attention to its raw distribution deal, Newman went into *Never Give An Inch* for director Richard A Colla. A clash of ideas soon became apparent and Newman was asked to step into the director's seat again. "I don't really regard it as my film," he says. "Colla had worked ten days, most of which footage I re-shot. I wasn't crazy about the idea of directing myself. It seemed like sticking a gun in my mouth. Still, I rang George Roy Hill and told him about my problem and he just got in his 'plane and flew up to where we were shooting and spent a week editing the logging sequence for me. He examined everything that Colla had got and told me what extra shots he thought I needed. Then he got back in his 'plane and flew back home again . . .''

If Newman tends to minimise his contribution to *Never Give An Inch*, he is simply bursting with pride about his film, *The Effects of Gamma Rays on Man-in-the-Moon Marigolds*. It stars Joanne Woodward as the unhappy, widowed mother of two girls (the Newmans' daughter Nell, and Roberta Wallach, daughter of Eli and Anne Jackson). "On *Rachel, Rachel* my involvement came about gradually, like the US involvement in Vietnam. It just grew and grew. But when I saw *Gamma Rays* as a play I knew straight off that I had to have it for Joanne. It never occurred to me that she might not want to play it. In the event, she hated the part, but I got around her. I think she's marvellous in the role. She looks dreadful, she seems to draw on some inner ugliness. Now she's making another film in which she looks like Garbo, just beautiful! There are some performances you can 'phone in, but not this one." Newman doesn't find directing his wife anything near the problem of directing himself: observers on the set report that they communicate like deaf-mutes using hands instead of dialogue. "The only snag was that Joanne tended to bring the character home at night, which was a bit of a pain in the arse. Nell was in *Rachel, Rachel* as well. She's not at all impressed with movies. The only reason she made this one was to earn money to feed her pigeons. She has pigeons, rabbits, a horse, a skunk, five dogs, one of which has just had five puppies. I refused to subsidise them any more, so she had to go out to work."

Newman's reputation as a hell-raiser may have been exaggerated, especially in latter years, but he is certainly a keen athlete and sportsman. Fast cars retain their appeal for him (he was able to indulge this hobby in the film *Winning*, just as Steve McQueen did in *Le Mans*). The days of motor-cycling, however, are definitely over. A bike accident a few years back left him in need of skin grafts on four fingers. "At first the doctors told me that I would never have the full use of my left hand again, that I would never be able to close it more than this." (He makes a weak half-fist.) "They suggested that I should practice by gripping a tennis ball but instead I took a wet towel and wrung it all day. In the mornings my hand would have frozen and the towel would be as thick as a man's arm, but by the evening I would get it squeezed so dry that my fist was nearly locked tight. If I have any problem like that, I go at it like a dog. I worry it till I've got it licked. If people would attack, if they would fight more, they'd stand a better chance. Now I have perfect use of the hand—look!" (a demonstration), "whereas the specialists say I should be partially paralysed. If you look at the early scenes in Alfred Hitchcock's *Torn Curtain* you will see that I am always carrying a coat over my arm. That's because the stitches were still visible.

Newman's sense of humour lies chiefly in the direction of practical jokes and confidence tricks, main butt of which is George Roy Hill—sometime friend, sometime enemy—his director on *Butch Cassidy & the Sundance Kid* and *The Sting*. Mention of Hill provokes a torrent of abuse. "That man is cheap. Not frugal, but cheap. He invited me over to his trailer for a drink one day. He drinks Scotch but I don't touch spirits any more. So he says, OK come over for a beer. When we get there he's out of both Scotch and beer, so I lend him some bottles from my trailer. Next day I bill him for eight dollars and ten cents and receive in reply a four-page, closely-typed letter talking about the abuse of our 'friendship quotient.' Well, I didn't get my money, so I went over to his office and cut his desk in half with a chain saw. He was really furious at the time, but then he nailed it together with three-by-one ply and went on using it. But wait." By now Newman has edged forward in his seat, certain of his audience and relishing the reliving of the story. "Next thing Universal sent me a bill for 437 dollars for one desk. So I send them a four-page closely-typed legal document saying that if I pay the bill, I shall charge them rent for the desk, since they are using it. They send me reminders saying 'Please pay this overdue amount now.' " It's good to know that, in the days of dwindling prosperity for the Hollywood studios, that Accounts Departments won't let go of the stray 437 dollars.

"George Roy has this old 'plane that takes ten days to fly across the country . . ." starts another hair-raising story of a pilot with back spasms and a motor that cuts out when the 'plane loops the loop. Newman gave Hill a model of it tangled in a treetop with the inscription: "To George Roy Hill, shot down by Vincent Canby and the critics." Newman and accomplice bungled a plan to cut Hill's Volkswagen in half with an oxyacetylene torch and dampers during the wrap party for *Slaughterhouse-Five*, but the 'plane is a perpetual temptation to Newman's bisecting talents. One feels that any project involving Hill, Newman and Redford is fraught with incipient dangers. A fencing bet on the *Butch Cassidy* set backfired when Newman's daughter warned Redford: "They're going to do something very bad to you," and one of the ring-leaders' wives threatened to leave him if he did anything dishonest like throwing the fight. Newman lost two dollars on that one and is as sore as hell. "Redford," he says with mock pomposity, "is not an honourable man . . ."

A shadow looms tall over Newman. "When I work for First Artists I get one hour for lunch. What is all this twelve-hour lunch crap?" asks Sidney Poitier.

"I'll let you into my secret, Good Lookin'," Newman replies. "I'm not working for First Artists."

GREGORY PECK

Covering the celebrations for Adolph Zukor's 100th birthday, "Paris-Match" referred to Gregory Peck as "the baby of the party at sixty-seven." Peck's outraged wife, Veronique, herself an ex-staff member of the magazine, cabled her displeasure: "My husband thanks you for the gift of ten years but, since they are in the wrong direction, he gives them back." Peck was, of course, fifty-seven, not sixty-seven ("At my age those ten years mean a lot. I think my wife was afraid that all her friends in Paris would think I had one foot in the grave.").

Since he all but gave up acting three years ago, Peck's dry humour has had to contend with repeated questioning about how it feels to be one of the Hollywood dinosaurs. He forces a smile and says through clenched teeth that it's "Oh, just terrible." He is a tall man, palpably fit, distinguishedly grey and blessed with an eloquence and rhetoric that have surely been cultivated over the years. One cannot really imagine him in the saddle, nor again as one of those frontier pioneers. The liberal lawyer of *To Kill a Mockingbird* (his Oscar-winning portrayal) is the easiest character to reconcile with this amiable, slowly-spoken man.

Certainly no dinosaur, certainly no anachronism. What, then, seems wrong as one encounters him behind a desk in the dingy, factory-canteen atmosphere of Elstree Studios? The scale is too small. It is as though some visiting dignatory has been accidentally delivered to the Town Hall instead of his four-star hotel. Yet it is a working environment and Peck is—always was—one of the working actors. He is here to supervise the final stages of post-production on *The Dove*, his own production about a lone mariner (Joseph Bottoms) who sailed the trade winds round the globe.

He is not dismayed by the drab uniformity of the studios (years ago he suffered agonies in the tank here as Ahab strapped to the back of *Moby Dick*; now he confesses, with a flicker of malice, that he half-enjoyed watching Bottoms taking the same punishment for *The Dove*.)

"Studios are much the same the world over," he says. "This is no different, except that it's very British. We had a very lachrymose afternoon when they had to drop half the personnel and all the chars who had been here since the year dot. Suddenly they were 'found to be redundant.' I suppose that is a frightfully British way of saying that they were fired. They got the point, all right. They spent the rest of the day wailing in the corridors."

Peck began to edge out of acting in the late '60s. "Everyone wants me to talk about the past, about the so-called 'golden' days of Hollywood. I was glad to be acting then, but in no way do I regret the passing of those times. Things are far more exciting now. I have a much greater capacity for looking forward than for looking back."

His production involvement had already begun with films like *Captain Newman M D, Pork Chop Hill, The Big Country, The Guns of Navarone, Cape Fear, To Kill a Mockingbird* and *Behold a Pale Horse* (in all of which he starred) but his first solo flight as a producer was with *The Trial of the Catonsville Nine*. It was an adaptation of a stage play about a group of everyday people who protested against the Vietnam War by burning draft records. "They laid their freedom on the line, possibly even their lives, for they were not to know how the police would behave." It was one of those quiet acts of courage that Peck so admires and he believed strongly that it should be seen by a wider audience. Unfortunately the film was not a commercial success and had no release in Britain.

"It ended up with a certain self-righteousness that the play never had," says Peck with commendable frankness. "It was all right playing night after night to the converted, but when it's a film you have to reach the barbarians as well. After five minutes, sections of the preview audience started to walk out."

He muses that the film might have been better received if it had carried the name of one of the well-known Hollywood political agitators. "Those people weren't around though," he says. "I don't think they even saw the film. I'm too old to be marching in the streets: it was my own protest against a war that I believed to be unjust. Politically it was the most incendiary film ever made in America. It's still smouldering, and mouldering, on the shelf."

Undeterred by the experience, Peck pressed ahead with plans for *The Dove*. Although these were well advanced, he took time out to act with Desi Arnaz Jnr in the western *Billy Two Hats*. Peck was resting at his house in Cap Ferrat when producer Norman Jewison and director Ted Kotcheff tried to interest him in Alan Sharp's script about two outlaws—a half-breed and an exiled Scot.

"It seemed a nice story, a pleasant look back over the shoulder at the difficult conditions under which our grandparents lived. And Ted seemed a wild, creative sort of person. Also, I couldn't resist the idea of doing a western in Israel." So Peck made an unexpected comeback. "I don't think you can

categorically give up something like acting. It's what I do, it's what I'm known for."

When he returned to *The Dove* (the title went full circle through "Once Upon a Painted Sea", "Here There Be Dragons" and back to *The Dove* again) casting was uppermost in his mind. He had seen Joe Bottoms in a television segment and thought he might be right for the role. He is the younger brother of Timothy Bottoms and there are yet another two—Sam, who played the retarded boy in *The Last Picture Show*, and Ben whom Peck reckons has the brightest future of them all. "They are an amazing family of California-Bohemians. They act, they make pottery, they sing, and suddenly they have these film star sons. I had asked Joe in to talk about the part and, of course, they all came and they all had opinions to contribute. But Joe was the most poetic, the most articulate: he had a real feeling about what motivates the character."

Deborah Raffin was similarly selected from a long line of young hopefuls. She had a Grace Kelly quality of stillness about her. "It was important, too, to find two people who looked right together. We had looked at all the elements in the story and decided that the love story was the most important. It's the girl who changes him from a boy into a man."

Under Charles Jarrott's direction, filming progressed peacefully ("He was very paternal and helpful to the actors: I sensed that when I saw *Anne of the Thousand Days.*") Peck kept in the background. "Sometimes I would compliment them if I thought they had done good work. But if things went wrong, I would talk to Charles about it, never to the kids directly."

Peck has five children of his own (from two marriages) and clearly enjoys the company of young people. "I have great sympathy for kids today, the drop-out generation. No wonder they are cynical. They find mendacity and corruption everywhere in the world. They cannot put their trust in their leaders as they have been taught. Even the air and the water around them is impure. They revolt and show their protest at the way the older generation has allowed the world to go to pot. Generally they come round in time. I watch my own children and I see their disillusionment in the world when they are forced to lose their ingenuousness and innocence. I cannot quarrel with the ways in which they might express their disappointment. I imagine it is very difficult to be idealistic as a young person today."

Gregory Peck (left) with Deborah Raffin and Joseph Bottoms, the stars of The Dove, and (right) with Mary Badham in his Oscar-winning film, To Kill a Mockingbird

On the other hand, Peck has great admiration for the younger generation's confidence and togetherness. "On *Billy Two Hats*, Desi was lying on the ground before the take and he suddenly said: 'What am I doing here? I'm a Cuban-Irish billionaire. Why am I lying in the dirt in the Israeli desert?' It's a good question. On *The Dove* I never ceased to wonder at Joe's confidence, but never more so than at that first audition. He came in, wearing dirty tennis shoes and blue jeans with holes in them and a non-descript shirt. I was amazed by his ease and confidence. When I was nineteen, I couldn't have done that.

"Producers were awesome figures in 900 dollar suits who went about in a cloud of cologne. Auditions always struck me dumb with terror."

JAMES STEWART

His voice conjures up phantoms from a rich and distinguished cinema past. Close your eyes and the years melt away: he is once more Mr Smith on his way to Washington; Mr Deeds; Mr Hobbs taking his vacation; the ordinary man championing decent values in a world where cynicism and corruption have a firm grip. The eyes twinkle, the face is weathered, otherwise he is just as one imagines: tall, gangling and inclined to stoop, the result of a lifetime of talking to shorter people and dodging low doorjams.

His conversation seems the result of deep thought and concentration. The drawl is distinctive: he snubs his consonants and pampers his vowels. He talks as though you have all the time in the world and nobody else to spend it with. And, in his amiably laconic presence, you have, and there isn't.

James Stewart was already an established star in the New York theatre when MGM approached him in the early '30s with a view to inviting him out to Hollywood. "There used to be a very extensive scouting programme for the movies," he explains. "MGM has an office in New York and they had seen quite a lot of my theatre work. I was asked to do a photographic test and then a scene from a play. Then they signed me up to three months as a contract artist. I didn't read the small print at the time, but the contract hasn't basically changed in fifty years. There are options—which mean they have a chance every three months to drop you if they like, but if they want to keep you, you are signed for seven years."

Stewart didn't leap into large parts straight away: small roles in films like Spencer Tracy's *The Murder Man* and the Jeanette MacDonald-Nelson Eddy *Rose Marie* gave him a chance to find his bearings and learn his craft in a strange place and a new industry. It is a time he recalls with affection and warmth and it was much later crystallised in his memory by making the film *Dynamite Man From Glory Jail*, which was set right at the heart of the Depression era. During those years the young James Stewart was himself struggling, to decide whether to try and follow through his training as a civil engineer and architect, or to give way to his yearning to become an actor. At Princeton, where he studied, he had been a member of Joshua Logan's university drama group and his fellow players had included Henry Fonda and Margaret Sullavan.

It was with his lifelong friend Fonda that he came to New York. "I really did want to become an architect but nobody was putting up buildings at the time. Yet the theatre was exploding: there was tremendous activity, a kind of reaction against the Depression. So many fine comedians were to develop in those years—Bob Hope, W C Fields, Bill Robinson. I think all my contemporaries would agree that we were particularly fortunate to have cut our teeth in the theatre at that time.

"When I get depressed by the solemnity of what is on the screen now, I talk to film makers and they say. 'There's nothing to laugh about in the world today.' Well, there certainly was nothing to laugh about then, either. They were very difficult times."

James Stewart came to Hollywood for three months and stayed for forty years. Clearly he came to love movies but it was, he says, a gradual process. There wasn't the time to do anything but the day's work, nor to be aware of much beyond it. "The big studios were an ideal training ground and one that has never been duplicated before or since. They really gave you the opportunity to learn your craft fully. At MGM they had forty or fifty contract players. We did small parts in pictures with stars like Myrna Loy, William Powell, Joan Crawford and Spencer Tracy, and then big parts in tiny pictures that were made in ten days.

"There was a whole department in the studio that was devoted to making B-features. That's where the Doctor Kildare and Andy Hardy series started. We were always very active. Not only were you under contract: you worked every day. For instance, there was another whole department that did nothing but make tests. It was an exciting, enormously stimulating experience."

The whole experience of being part of the studio star system in those years must have been like playing in a vast game of Monopoly. "The studio would trade us like baseball players. Almost half of the movies I did up to the war were made for other studios. They would barter, sometimes trade an actor, a story, a director or a property, even the use of a studio facility. This was all part of the game. MGM had this roster of people—the Barrymores, Garbo, Norma Shearer, Jean Harlow—that's why they were Top Dog. Warners had Cagney, Bette Davis, Bogart, Jane Wyman—but they tended to keep people rather than trade."

During his formative years as a film actor, Stewart was working with a number of talents, in front of and behind the camera, who are today revered as artists but were then just part of the studio's assets. He admits to being too engrossed with what he was doing himself always to spot them. But directors

James Stewart in his most recent film, Dynamite Man from Glory Jail

like George Cukor, Ernst Lubitsch and Frank Capra are the three Stewart selects as being recognisably, tangibly of a different calibre. "I always had the feeling of something special when I was working with them. One thing they all had in common was the ability to put a story on the screen with vitality and excitement. This entailed a lot of things, but primarily an understanding of the camera. They all used the medium as it should be used: the visuals came first, and then the dialogue. They all felt that if they couldn't make their point visually, then something was wrong. This was not the case with a lot of people: they were so impressed by the fact that the screen could talk that they tended to imitate the stage and rely on the spoken word. I have always felt that this was wrong."

Until the war Stewart stayed with MGM and swiftly graduated to bigger and better parts. He won his Oscar (surprisingly his only one) for *The Philadelphia Story* in which he starred with Katharine Hepburn and Cary Grant. But before that had come the image-making *Mr Smith Goes to Washington* and Lubitsch's *The Shop Around the Corner*. The outbreak of war interrupted a career in top gear. His seven-year contract with MGM still had eighteen months to run and, as things then stood, he would have to return to the studio at the end of the war and complete the contract (probably at the same salary). Bette Davis had tried a legal stand

against this particular aspect of tyranny within the contract system, but it was the de Havilland decision (*q.v.*) which directly affected Stewart. The courts ruled that the years specified in a contract must be served consecutively and if, for any reason, there was an interruption (in the cases of the Misses Davis and de Havilland by dint of their refusal to play the mediocre parts offered by the studios, and their subsequent suspensions) those years could no longer be added to the end of the contract time. So for Stewart the end of the war brought a professional freedom. He has never since been under contract to a studio again, preferring to work as a freelance.

His first film after the war was for his beloved Capra and it remains his favourite to this day: *It's a Wonderful Life.* He played the owner of a small-town building society driven to attempt suicide by the loss of a large sum of money which will make him look like a criminal fraud. At the moment of suicide he is visited by an elderly angel who shows him his town and his friends as they would have been if he had not been born to help and make his mark on them. Sobered by this vision and the sudden realisation that his life has not been as useless as he had hitherto thought, he rushes home to his family and the happiest of endings.

"I was interested to read in Capra's book (which, by the way, is excellent) that it is his favourite, too.

James Stewart croons "Easy To Love" to Eleanor Powell in the 1936 musical Born To Dance

Left: James
Stewart in
Firecreek.
Above: on
the MGM
backlot
filming the
linking
narrative for
That's
Entertainment

I have known Frank for forty years and only recently discovered that. All the great directors of that age had a tendency to look for the original, not the film of the play or the film of the book. Frank Capra got the idea for *It's a Wonderful Life* from a Christmas card someone sent him. The inscription read: 'Everyone does something in his life, and it helps for everyone to have been born'—something like that. That one line gave him the idea for the whole picture.

"I remember that, years ago at MGM, there was a man called Hopkins. He was probably listed as a writer, but he was really an ideas man, I don't think he ever went into his office all day long. I would always see him walking, walking, walking about the lot, just dreaming up ideas for films . . ."

Greatest of all the "ideas men" Stewart has worked with is Alfred Hitchcock and, during his middle period, the actor was the quintessential Hitchcock hero in films like *The Man Who Knew Too Much, Rope, Rear Window* and *Vertigo*. "Hitch is as thoroughly prepared as anyone I have ever worked with. His knowledge of the camera is most impressive. I've always claimed that, if you wanted to try, you could recite the telephone directory and, if he liked the scene visually, he would keep it in the film. But he's a nightmare to a script clerk. She'll keep coming over to him and saying: 'It's not right,' and he'll say: 'But did you *understand?*' and most of the time the poor thing will have to say yes.

"I remember when I was in England making *The Man Who Knew Too Much*. There was a scene in which I had been knocked over the head and locked in a church. When I regained consciousness I had to climb up the bellrope. I said to Hitch: 'That doesn't make sense, why don't I just break a window to get out? He said: 'But if you did that, you would be out, and you wouldn't have climbed the rope or rung the bell . . .' To him this was a complete explanation and justification for the scene."

He would welcome the opportunity to work with younger directors and to be exposed to new techniques. Incredibly, nobody has yet asked him. "The new directors are very aware of visuals. Some of them attack it—I won't say in the *wrong* way—but in a way I don't find as effective as the

Fords, the Capras and the Clarence Browns. In the old days, when the western makers got a script from the front office, the first thing they did was to weigh it. If it was too heavy they would cut it. Only later would they get around to reading it." He recalls an incident when the Lux Theatre of the Air wanted to do a sixty-minute radio adaptation of one of his westerns, and were baffled and finally defeated by the fact that they couldn't find any dialogue.

Since the drop in the number of comedy scripts in circulation, Stewart's forte has been the western, in which genre he has worked with Ford, Anthony Mann and, more recently, Andrew V McLaglen, the director of *Dynamite Man From Glory Jail*. He explains the link-up with McLaglen: "I had seen some of his television work and heard about him from John Ford, with whom he served his apprenticeship. He tells stories of being on the set even as a tiny child when his father, Victor McLaglen, was making *The Informer* for Ford. Anyway, he uses the camera the same way as Ford, he has the same feeling for getting vitality and excitement on the screen. That's why I like him."

With McLaglen, Stewart has made *Shenandoah, The Rare Breed* and *Bandolero!*, all within the western genre. *Dynamite Man From Glory Jail* was something of a departure in that it followed the adventures of three released prisoners during the Depression years. The attempts to go straight are hampered by a bunch of "responsible" citizens more crooked and more sinister than any behind bars. "It was such a pure, honest story," says Stewart, who personally got the script off a shelf at a rival studio and into production. "The good guys against the bad guys: pure melodrama."

Stewart recently returned, via Canadian television, Broadway and then the London stage, to the role with which he is most readily associated—the befriender of the invisible six-foot rabbit in *Harvey*. "It was interesting to me that the younger audiences took it, not as an escape from reality, but as a confrontation of reality." He continues: "Suddenly I find that my old pictures are re-opening at regular movie theatres and doing great business.

"I guess I must have become a collector's piece."

INDEX

The Films Illustrated Team

DAVID CASTELL (Editor) was educated at the Century, Clapham Junction, where was hatched the idea of the magazine. After a mis-spent youth, he wrote on the cinema for *London Life, The Illustrated London News* and *The Times Educational Supplement*. In 1969 he co-founded Films in London Publications

SUSAN d'ARCY (Assistant Editor) contributes to *The Sunday Telegraph* and various women's magazines. She is co-author of *The Films of Dirk Bogarde* (LSP) and has just completed *The Films of Peter Finch* in the same series. Before joining *Films Illustrated*, she was a feature writer and reviewer for *Photoplay*

JOHN WILLIAMS (Associate Editor) was a co-founder of Films in London Publications and has since been closely involved with the development of *Films Illustrated*. He was born in Wales in 1944 and spends most of his free time growing begonias and other odd plants. He is increasingly concerned with the conservation of our natural environment

Notes on Contributors

MARGARET HINXMAN is the film critic of *The Daily Mail*. Born in South London, she has been addicted to films from an early age. After three years as film critic of *Time & Tide* she joined *Picturegoer* as a feature writer and later film reviewer. After the demise of *Picturegoer* she became the film reviewer for the trade paper *The Daily Cinema*. She was film critic of *Queen* for four years and of *The Sunday Telegraph* for seven years until 1974 when she joined *The Daily Mail*. She is co-author of *The International Encyclopedia of Film* (Michael Joseph) and *The Films of Dirk Bogarde* (LSP)

TOM HUTCHINSON is film critic of *The Sunday Telegraph* and science fiction reviewer of *The Times*. Married with three children and a bizarrely beautiful cat called Ben, he lives in North London from where he assiduously pursues his favourite hobbies — watching films and reading science fiction. He regards SF as a marvellous literary mechanism for commenting on human nature and aspirations

but is, himself, so unscientific he cannot even mend a fuse

CLYDE JEAVONS, one-time journalist and stagehand, is Deputy Curator of the National Film Archive and author of three books in Hamlyn's "Pictorial History" series: *War Films, Westerns* (with Michael Parkinson) and *Sex in the Movies* (with Jeremy Pascall). He writes regular monthly film columns for the magazines *She* and *Look Now*, contributes spasmodically to *The Monthly Film Bulletin, Sight and Sound* and *Films Illustrated*,

DAVID QUINLAN has been reviewing and writing about films since he was eighteen which he has to admit was seventeen years ago. Born in London, and educated at St Dunstan's College, he now lives in Kent with a wife, three children and a cat named Stanley. Film writer for *TV Times*, he contributes to a number of other magazines. He believes that the cinema must put entertainment above all other factors if it is to survive as a mass medium

KENNETH THOMPSON was born in Croydon in 1926. He joined the Cinematograph Exhibitors' Association in 1948 as trade film critic and remained there until the demise of the publication in 1971. He has also contributed reviews to *The Monthly Film Bulletin* and *Films Illustrated*. He "dabbles" in musicology and is the author of *A Dictionary of 20th Century Composers* (Faber & Faber) and *The Works of Arthur Bliss* (Novello). He estimates that he has reviewed about 6,000 films during his career

ADRIAN TURNER was born in 1947 and joined the staff of the Everyman Cinema, Hampstead in 1970. Since 1973 he has been in control of the Everyman's programmes. He is film critic of *The Hampstead and Highgate Express* and contributes regularly to *Films Illustrated*

Acknowledgments

Independent Magazines (Publishing) Limited acknowledges the help of Avco-Embassy; Columbia; EMI; Lion International; MGM; Paramount; The Rank Organisation; 20th Century-Fox; United Artists; Universal; Walt Disney. And, as always, a special debt of gratitude to the Book Library and Information Department of The British Film Institute